Island Writings

A unique collection from 14 islands off the coast of Ireland

GW00801891

Cover artwork by Nonie O'Neill

Published by
Womens Interisland Network
(W.I.N.)

© Womens Interisland Network
(W.I.N.) 2007

ISBN 978-0-9556620-0-3

Typeset by Artwerk, Dublin

Printed and bound by Betaprint, Dublin, Ireland

D' oileánaigh ar fud an domhain mhóir
— To islanders everywhere!

Acknowledgements

Many thanks to the staff of Comhdháil Oileáin na hÉireann for all their support in compiling this collection and to Irene Graham for her invaluable professional input. Caitlín and Máire from the Irish translation company Cleas and the editing committee deserve great credit for their contribution. Thanks also to Sabrina Verdecampo McCarron, Nonie O'Neill, Kitty Rooney Sullivan, Rachel Burke, Stephanie Brennan and Olwen Gill for tying it all together and last but by no means least, a very special thanks to all the authors who allowed their work to be published.

Index

Forward

Islands by their very nature are special places and this unique collection of work, by 34 women from 14 different islands, provides a rare and wonderful insight into the ways and wanderings of island life. The voices are young and old and reflect some of the history, mystery and magic, together with the sheer beauty of Ireland's islands. We hope that the enthusiasm expressed by the authors in putting this collection together, will encourage readers to come and immerse themselves in our rich cultural heritage to experience at first hand, the rhythms of nature in harmony with twenty first century living.

This is Ireland's first inter-island collection of reflections, musings, poetry and prose, it is a fantastic first step which will hopefully encourage many more islanders to put pen to paper and share their thoughts in future publications. Enjoy!

An excerpt from **Katie's Dance**
Ruth Alden, Oileán Chléíre

Bell pealing. Final prayer over. School Master Dan at the door shaking her hand as she prepared to set off into the summer of 1899.

"No more incomplete sentences, young lady," he said, "For they indicate incomplete thought. You know what a blacksmith is. You're a wordsmith." He'd a ritual of giving every student a tip to ponder over the holidays.

As part of her own ritual, Katie stepped outside, kicked off shoes, slipped them into her lunch box and darting round classmates, set off on the mile run home. Sure, sharp stones hurt. Sure, classmates laughed at her, called out "Where's the fire?" "Who's the man?" "Is the Last Judgement at hand?" But her feet toughened up on that initial run, not that she didn't skip over cowpats and avoid occasional shards of glass. No bother.

Two weeks later she could stub out a cigarette anywhere on either sole. The joy of calluses. But what she really valued she couldn't explain: that sense of freedom; that sense that one world of rigorous discipline was shifting into another of challenging fun. Some days she'd help her father tend the hay, or build the mother cocks; some days help her mammy pack the week's catch of pilchard into hogsheads to squeeze out oil for tilly lamps; some days she'd give her brothers a pre-breakfast break by milking the eleven cows – in alphabetical order, Aileen, Betsy, Emir… She'd a good knack with the teats, and if any siblings dropped by, she could squirt a stream of milk into the face across the narrow byre.

End of July, soles hard as horseshoes, along comes cousin Danny. He relates how out lobstering, he'd recently chatted across a short stretch of lumpy sea with a stonemason working on the eighth bottom half-course of the new Fastnet Lighthouse. When Danny learned how bored the workers were with tinned beans and dried sausage, he returned with twenty-four chops from a cow he'd just slaughtered. The men on the Rock heard him fiddling with his accordion while they coughed up their shilling and sixpence. As they lowered him the coins in a small burlap bag, they invited him, his accordion and any others – especially unmarried young ladies – to a Sunday afternoon party, weather permitting.

"So, Katie girl, might we get together four or five girls and pay them a visit?" Then the surprise. "Celebrate your eighteenth with a splurge? This Sunday!"

Despite her connection to the Lighthouse, Katie'd never been on the Rock. Since she'd turned four, the Fastnet'd been significant in her life. Her father, fishnets spread beside the house, had repeatedly teased her by saying, "Katie girl, go out and tell us the weather." When she'd re-enter the house, she'd sometimes report, "There is no weather."

"The Rock? Why," she shared with Danny, "when I'd step outside my left ear was east, my right ear the Fastnet. I learned to read the weather."

"You'll join me?" asked Danny. "And arrange for a few lassies?"

"Cousin! Consider this affair one done deal."

Two hours later, her four closest friends had agreed to join her at Duffy's pier after Sunday dinner. The thought of visiting what she'd looked out at all her life gave her a chilly thrill. The thought of dancing with men she'd never met intensified a growing ambivalence.

The day came.

The birthday breakfast.

The half-hour walk to Church.

The prayers for the Boer War to be over.

The family dinner.

Mid-afternoon they cast off the ropes, rowed Danny's thirty-foot *Blue Jacket* – with Katie pulling flood oar – out the harbour mouth, hoisted sail. Katie stowed oar under gunwale, sat straddling stem-post with bare lower legs and feet dangling. Now and then a breaking bow wave wet lower appendages but she liked the feel of seawater dribbling down legs.

At first, the Fastnet seemed to grow no nearer but after an hour she began to sense it looming.

"You all right, Katie?" asked Danny. "Your toes're twitching."

"Getting ready."

"You mean you're nervous."

"I mean – Look, there, on the steps beside the short tram line –"

"Yes, cuz, men. All those ties flapping in the breeze. And now," Danny called out, "lower sails. Drop anchor. Let out rope as we row to the landing. Once we've climbed into the net and been lifted up and tossed our bow rope to the men so that they can secure us to a bollard, Jack here can pull *Blue Jacket* back to our stern anchor.

"Okay, ladies, you five in the first load. When the basket comes down, and the slow swell lifts us up next to it, you tumble into net. Here comes. In with ye." The girls jumped. Soon a man was offering Katie his hand to help her up. She leapt, came down hard onto bare feet, shouted, "Let the dance begin!"

She and Chloé, as quickly out of the net as herself, joined hands and swung each other around. Next they knew, they were flying around in circles. The six men there to greet them broke into applause. Hearing a creaking above them, Katie and Chloé stopped. All watched the basket pick up Danny and Connie and deposit them on the landing.

Cuddy then gave a formal welcome, introduced his colleagues and two lighthouse keepers, and had Danny introduce the young women and crew. Next Cuddy led them up the stone steps to the flat area east of lighthouse base. There stood a table filled with sausages and tins of plums, cracker biscuits, a jar of pickles, a platter of carrots. Danny sat down with back against the tower and warmed up his box, called out, "Eight to every dance, with change of partners every time too, and then everybody'll get to know everybody. We'll start with some Cape Clear sets, two opposite two and polish those slides. Men to the left of their partners."

Katie began with Dineen, but shortly partner passed partner to new partner. Yes, she thought, the Fastnet's not just a place to look at but also a place to *be*.

For the next dance Katie, the odd one out, settled down beside Danny, tucked loose folds of pleated twill cotton dress between knees and concentrated on male feet. She'd never watched black leather shoes dancing before and was amazed at how different feet communicated different personalities, some light and spirited, others heavy and determined, others confused and questioning. Then she thought of someone watching her feet dance, she the only barefoot participant.

Cuddy sat down on the other side of Katie and introduced himself.

"Goodness," Katie exclaimed, "your hand's as callused as my feet. Do you walk the Rock on your hands?"

He laughed and explained: "With these hands I examine every ashlar[1]. Check particularly where the joins take place, the dove-tail areas."

"So your hands are tough but sensitive. And you haven't danced yet," Katie commented.

---

1 Masonry made of large square-cut stones

"Not yet. I'm married, father of four. Maybe a dance near the end. Just watching this event's a healthy change of pace."

Danny brought dance to end, announced,

"Next dance a bit faster. Then refreshment time."

Stonemason Jason stood before Katie bowed. "My lady, may I have this dance?"

"I'd be honoured," she replied, but wondered what she was getting into, for Jason had a gorilla build and bulging eyes. His nose took a sharp left turn near its tip. His eyebrows reminded her of furry black caterpillars. His shoes had been among the confused and questioning. The dance started slowly. Jason swung Katie round with such power she discovered she had to turn her head in advance of the swirl or else she'd lose balance.

Danny shifted into a rambunctious waltz that didn't remain a waltz long. The formality, the pattern, the sliding all disappeared. Skirts swirled, ties flapped, hats lifted, arms and legs swung about. Katie imagined them all as butterflies. They darted around each other, twisting and turning the women pirouetting, the men wildly opening their arms, shaking their wings. Danny's squeezebox reached a crescendo, ended with long-held chord.

Silence.

Bass growl.

Butterflies tumbling down.

"Break time . . . but first an announcement," called out Cuddy. "Robert, the little surprise, please. There's the largest cake ever concocted on Charraig Aonair. Excuse the lack of candles, for we've enough candle power here already."

"Ladies and gentlemen," announced Danny, "this dance'll be the last, as the sun's only half an hour left. All five women, and you men without a partner, cut in regularly. Keep them feet asliding."

"May I have *this* dance then, Miss Katie?" asked Dineen. Katie accepted his hand. When the music ended, Katie had danced with seven butterflies.

The Wake on Gola Island in 1962
Kathleen Brady, Aranmore

There's been a terrible tragedy we were told in Aranmore
Young Michael McGinley and a Scots girl found dead upon the shore.
On Gola Island to the north, they were trapped under the curragh
"We must go to wake the dead," said Jack the Glen.

"You know his sisters well," said Jack "You too must come along."
Such a sad sail north that afternoon, no whistle or a song.
I remember Philly steering and the silent boat of men,
"It is good to wake the dead," said Jack the Glen.

As little isle came into sight an eerie sound was heard.
It seemed to float across the waves like strange calls of the sea bird.
I turned in alarm to look around at the ululating sound,
"They are keening for the dead," said Jack the Glen.

Before the house of mourning was a long, low, whitewashed wall
There the grieving island women sat, each wrapped in her black shawl.
As our boat was tied up at the slip, the wailing rose and fell.
"God help them in their grief," said Jack the Glen.

The McGinley sisters greeted us, their friends from Aranmore
They cried out and they hugged us as we stepped across the floor
Chairs were pulled around the fire, tea and drinks were poured for those
Who had come to wake the dead with Jack the Glen.

I can ne'er forget the scenes I saw that summer afternoon,
Or the sight of their dead brother laid out in the upper room.
Such a young, dark, handsome man in brown scapular and shroud
"Let us all kneel down and pray," said Jack the Glen.

"Why did he have to go, he was all we had!" they cried
But only God knows why such a fine young man had died.
We hoped our prayers would help them, but our hearts were oh, so sad.
As we sailed back from the wake with Jack the Glen.

Men of Donegal
Kathleen Brady, Aranmore

God fashioned very special men
To live in the north-west
Dauntless, strong and full of pride
They had to be His best

He knew the dangers they could face
Strong spirits hard to break
No matter where they had to go
This spirit they would take

They needed it when down the pits
In Scotland's gloomy mines
They needed it when in the States
They laid the railway lines

From east to west and north to south
And o'er the globe they went
And to their homes in Donegal
Their hard-earned money sent

Their steadfast faith they took with pride
And kept it burning bright
Though many hardships they might face
Their prayers were said each night

This faith they taught and nurtured well
To many generations
And St. Patrick's hymn was often sung
To people of all nations

Now when we're asked where we've come from
With pride we stand so tall
To say we're all descended from
The men of Donegal

Donegal Women's Network
Kathleen Brady, Aranmore

Women here, women there,
Women, women everywhere.
Busy taking care of all,
Especially here in Donegal.

And then one day there came some news.
Would women meet and air their views?
They met – the Women's Network came,
Life would never be the same!

Coffee mornings, evening classes,
Painting stones and painting glasses.
Dressmaking and icing cakes,
Painting scenes of hills and lakes.

Bewildered husbands scratched their heads.
"Decoupage? What's that?" they said.
"Wait and see," replied their wives,
The Network's brightened up our lives.

No tired, bored wives around the houses,
But bright and attractive to their spouses.
The Women's Network transformed all,
We'll keep it here in Donegal.

Danny

Kathleen Brady, Aranmore

There are many sad stories connected with Aranmore Island, and one of them concerned my own people in 1907. It was the month of June and the weather was beautiful. Jimmy Grainne Rodgers, my great grandfather, was off to the mainland for the day, but left instructions for all the jobs that were to be completed before he returned. The eldest sons, Paddy and Jimmy, were busy threshing corn on a slab near the house, so the father told the middle boys Mickie Jimmy and Fran, to finish their tasks around the little farm before taking the large brown cow up to the pasture on the mountain. The youngest boy, Danny who was eleven years of age, wanted to join the others. However, Jimmy Grainne said no, he was too young and must stay around the house to be of any help to his mother or his sisters, Kate and Grace. He could draw water from the well or keep the fire going with the turf while the women baked and prepared meals. Danny was not pleased. The morning passed until it was time for the brothers to set off for the mountain and Danny pleaded with his mother to let him accompany them. Eventually, Jimmy Beag the second eldest brother, assured the mother the boy could come to no harm – what danger or problem could there be with four older boys to look out for him?

The boys enjoyed their afternoon up on the pasture. As the cow grazed they lay in the heather talking about school, their friends, their oldest brother Paddy's recent marriage to the priest's housekeeper. Then cheery shouts rang out and they were joined by two of their friends who had brought a battered old ball. They tossed and kicked it around for another hour until the cow's lowing reminded them it was time to be off home. The cow had been tethered with a long thick rope so Mickie untied it preparing to go.

Danny wanted the job of leading the cow down, never having done it before. He shouted and jumped around Mickie who at last agreed and wound the thick rope round and round Danny's thin shoulder and upper arm. Just as they turned down the passageway, there was a loud clap of thunder. The boys had not noticed the change in the weather and all eyes turned skywards. The poor cow however, taking fright at this loud noise began to gallop down the passageway. Danny ran trying to keep up, but the impetus of the cow's dash was too much for the little boy. He lost his footing and being attached to the cow with the rope still round his arm, he was dragged for many yards. His little head and body were battered on the rocks, and only when he became wedged between two large boulders did the cow slow down, and then stopped. The others rushing and slipping behind, sobbed and cried as they looked down at the little body huddled by the rocks. Mickie unwound the last of the rope, while the others ran to the nearest house for help. Men came running with blankets and tenderly carried the broken little boy to Greene's house. The priest and doctor were sent for but no one could help – Danny had been battered to death on the rocks.

When Jimmy Grainne returned from Burtonport, he was told the awful news and brought to Greene's house. Beside himself with grief, he walked from room to room carrying the pitiful little body still wrapped in blankets. For hours he would not part with the child, until his broken-hearted wife, Kate, pleaded with him to bring their child down home to be prepared for burial. The whole island grieved over the loss of little Danny. The family's grief was partly assuaged five months later when the wife of the oldest son Paddy, gave birth to their first child. He was a healthy baby boy who was given the name of Danny – named for the dead boy. This baby was to be my father.

Portán

Stephanie Brennan, Inis Mór

We place a crustacean
flailing,
In the wrinkled sand.
Shiftily he disappears,
Crab (apple) jam.

You are impatient
(It's raining),
Holding in your hand,
That which I'm to Latinise
Being what I am.

I do not know the answer
Nor do I care in place as this.
The waves, mighty tympani
To water rush at kiss.

Corr Éisc

Stephanie Brennan, Inis Mór

Long, stock still stick,
Harsh shriek, shrill call,
Quick stab, sharp beak,
Ardea Cinerea.

Léarscáil

Stephanie Brennan, Inis Mór

Let me turn explorer,
Call up cartographers
To brindlemap
Your stippleback
Raised river veins
And gorsen plains.

Let me trace 'dentations,
Crenellations
Beam broadness,
Rough hewn hands
Downy *pinnae*
Shaleshingle sands.

Let me tread,
Trundle,
Trample,
Trek
And be cast exhausted on
The shoulder shore
That is neck.

A Journey From Belfast To Aran
Mary Burke, Inis Mór

Six of us were living outside Belfast and worked together in a factory. We read a newspaper advert looking for workers for a factory in Greenford, Middlesex, England. We decided to apply and after a week we got word back. We took off for England. The contract was just for six weeks, as it was up to ourselves if we wanted to stay there longer. The first three weeks, three of them were crying with homesickness – remember we were young women in our middle to late twenties. After five weeks, the other five decided to go back home, but I said I would stay longer. After all, it was only six weeks, not six years. So I saw them off to the train on a Friday evening and plucked up my courage the next evening and went to an Irish Dance Hall on my own. That was when I met my Waterloo. It was some meeting as we did not have a clue what either of us were saying, as Pat, a native Irish speaker had broken English and I had my strong Northern accent! At any rate we persevered, otherwise I would not be here telling the tale.

We were married in my local chapel at home in the North, and two months later I was travelling to Aran, off the coast of Galway, a six-hour journey on the steamer to Inis Mór. It was certainly a completely new world to me, especially when that northeast wind was blowing. It was an experience I never forgot and I still hate that northeast wind. I vowed then, I would never live here. Picture no ESB, no cinemas, no sanitation – I felt I could never settle.

The loneliness was heartbreaking for me. My poor old mother would send me parcels of tea and sugar etc. I would write to her, "Ma, it's not a desert island I'm living on." Anyway, she wrote: "Mary love, if you could get a little place and do Bed and Breakfast, they could go to Galway for their dinner." "Yes," I replied, "but they would have to swim thirty miles to Galway." "Oh Lord," she said, "I forgot about the sea."

And of course, there was no tourism in those days. In time I settled down to rear six children. It was certainly difficult, but it was a more peaceful and innocent time. The kids made their own fun and games. It was a great treat for them to get a trip to Galway. I did not get to visit my home again for eight long years, and travelling with five children was a bit of a nightmare, but we always got there and back safely enough. Children today could not imagine our life back then – no TV, no entertainment, no cars or buses and maybe waiting for three weeks for the steamer to travel with provisions. Trying to bake bread was the bane of my life.

We did have some laughs. I reckon that my sense of humour sustained me through a lot of hard times.

The West's Awake
Rachel Burke, Inis Mór

The West's awake
And who woke her?
Was it Brendan Behan
And his noisy Borstal Boys?
Or was Yeats
Calling from the grave?
Did the cannons from Easter Monday
Interrupt her slumber?
Or was it Limerick's Walls
Pounding at the crossroads?
Maybe the Night of the BigWind
Uprooting her turf – frightened her
Or did a lamenting Banshee
Appear with a warning for Roisín Dubh?
Did she hear the strong manly forms
In their chorus of 'Glory O'?

And now awoken
Does she note the corncrakes' absence?
And the wooden clicks of Mary
Through rheumatic hands at nine
And that rhythm of the churn
Then slapping butter into shape?
Is her land less sacred
Now the Mass has gone indoors?
Does she miss the children learning gaeilge in the hedge?
Or the sight of red báinín sails
Blowing amongst the homemade grey dividers
Against the rough blue Atlantic?
Does it cut her to the quick
To hear Kevin Barry on the whistle?
And no jingle jangle along the Royal Canal?

Now the history of horse's journeys
Lie under her smooth roads
And her free running rivers
Nourish her diseased blackened skin
That fed the poor man death
Did she sleep to forget
Her plunder of her people?

Stones of Aran
Rachel Burke, Inis Mór

Voices of old
Leak from the stones
"An-lá."
"Tá sé gaofar inniu."
Flat walls that once held families, chickens and traditions
Sara Mac Dara rushing her kids out to Mass
"Déan deifir. Ná bí deireanach."
Tommy Cole Nan tucking his trousers into his socks before cycling
to Kilronan
"Tá an bád ag teacht."
Gap stones worn smooth
Micheál and his son at dawn going fishing
"Go'le[1] a mhac."
Bartley Jamesie settling his speck hat on his smooth head before
walking the mile to the pub
"Beidh pionta agam. Beidh mé abhaile don tae."
Horses hooves and shoes made of cowhide
On the roads made from broken stones of grey
Scrógaí agus ronnachaí buí left on tops of the walls to dry
Shirts and trousers amuigh ar an gclaí
Sheets spread wide on fuchsia hedges
"Tabhair isteach cúpla fata ón ngarraí."
Mairín shouts out to Peadar
Cat mór dubh
Ina chodladh ar an sconsa.

---

1 Gabh i leith – come here

The Stations
Katherine Conneely, Inis Oírr

We filed out of the darkness,
Found seats, sat in silence,
Neighbours nodding to each other,
Men in hallway, behind the door,
Whispers.
A flaming fire, a shining house,
White table-clothed altar,
Last flowers of a dead summer
Priest in white, silver chalice
Inscribed 1845, reflected him,
Reflected us, all in one reflection.
When he mentioned it, we remembered
The harshness of history,
The happiness of here.
Friends, neighbours, family gathered
In a silver chalice
Shimmering,
In the wine of celebration
And the blood of sacrifice,
All the years between.
We looked at the young faces
Of our own returned emigrants,
The fresh ones, not seventeen
So much has changed since
First mass reflected in that chalice
And yet,
Not much

Thorny Garden of Eden
Katherine Conneely, Inis Oirr

Not for me dull sodden land
Disturbed by upcroppings
Of white thorny mayflower
And yellow spiked heather
With cattle splurging their way home.
But for me a place
With white rocky back glistening
Under the raw red setting sun.
A hump backed stranded island
Amid sparkling sea and shimmering sky.
A mere bone of earth
Keeping itself afloat
While stripping me of unnecessaries.
A keeper of spring gentian and campion
Storm stranded sparrow hawk,
Arctic tern and sun seeking swallow.
Yes, for me this sun faded picture
Of bleached rock, bleached sand and sky
That I can touch and see and feel and know
With the sureness of earthly instinct
That in this thorny garden of Eden
Is all that is life to me.

Summer Slumber
Katherine Conneely, Inis Oírr

I'm drunk on drowsiness
While Lord Cat sleeps in chair
Not minding swallows sweep
The dead, dusty air.

Jet paints a white line
In a blue frosted sky.
Boats on a glazed sea
Like life, pass me by.

Currachs curved and black
Hauling towards the land.
Silhouetted seagulls slumber
Beyond sun scorched sand.

I'm drunk on drowsiness
Summer sounds in the air,
Lost in a sultry slumber
While Lord Cat sleeps in chair.

Ancient Ways
Katherine Conneely, Inis Oírr

The ancient ways are going
For the old woman knows words
In Gaelic, her grandchildren don't,
Their Irish, modern, anglicised,
Hers bound to the earth
Carved by it as the rock underfoot.
The currachs like discarded shells
Of black backed beetles
Lie rotting in the sand.
The well-worn paths once woven
Into the landscape by feet
Are now mudded and gouged by tractor
Tyres no longer bordered
By smooth, soft margins,
Once home to wild garlic and primrose.
The Arctic Tern still finds a shelter
As does the Cuckoo and the Swallow
But the Corncrake left long ago.
Grey rock, grey sand, grey sky
Still the same, not yet scarred
But there's a change in the wind
For the ancient ways are going,
Blowing away.

Did the Boat Go Out?
Marie Coyne, Inisbofin

Did the boat go out?
What's the day like?

Think will there be a second boat?
What will I do?
Will I wait 'till the evening?

The forecast is bad
The day is getting worse.

The harbour's mouth is broken right across,
The sea fell with the last shower.

Once he gets a few miles out he'll be grand
The tide and wind will be with him coming in.

Oh, forget about the evening
The tide will be going back against the wind.

You have the best part of the day with you now
So if I were you I'd make for Cleggan.

They won't wait around today
So don't waste any time.

There is a big swell, but not much wind yet
There is no good on the sun though.

They had a job trying to hold the boat in Cleggan yesterday
There was an awful run on the tide.

If you don't get in today, God knows when you will get in;
The forecast for the whole week is bad.

Inishark
Marie Coyne, Inisbofin

Tranquil sea, sparkling gently in the sun,
Gives me a feeling that everything is alright,
Until my eyes drift to the black
Door and windowless houses, on the land of Shark.

For those who let you know decay,
I can safely say, sometimes I feel sad for them,
For they did not know how to love you
And keep you safe for another day.

Now still and quiet lying where you have always been.
In the midst of thorns, briars, nettles and sheep trodden grass
Your buildings fall stone by stone
Until another wall is gone.

Grassy steps lead to a door-less jamb,
While lilies bloom along the wall
Living and loving life in the sun,
Just like the dandelion on the roof.

Old purple slates slide to the ground
To let the outside in, or the inside out,
Rafters bare, half stripped of slate stand alone,
For there is no gable.

Damp green ceiling boards
Rot and fall from rusty nails
Scattered in disarray about the room
For this is their tomb.

Through a door built of stone, the sun shines,
While a two-legged table, slants to the floor.
Bottles, bare bedsprings, old shoes and cooking pots
Lie about the ground.

Green moss grows around the chimney
Where black soot once had its day.
Piles of slates and tiles are stacked where a fireside chair
Once rocked as neighbours talked.

A frightened sheep with maggots peers
From a bedroom door, then hurries to the other side
Forgetting the agony in the back,
A human is more a threat, though maggots will cause her death.

St. Leo's church stands roofless, doorless and windowless
Two crosses crown the gables.
They still praise the sky in sun and rain
As the wind howls by.

St. Leo's well is overgrown with weeds
It reflects my sad face
Though I find this to be a beautiful,
Spiritual and peaceful place.

The schoolyard seems to be the quietest of all
I think I should hear children's voice
As they run and shriek with screams of delight
Enjoying their play till teacher calls.

The old boat winches
And the rails around the harbour wall
Are brown with rust, there is no pier at all
Only a broken up wall.

St. Leo's cemetery at the cliff top rests
Stones at top and bottom mark the graves,
But there is no one now to name these graves
That are greeted daily by the waves.

In 1960 your people left
Because the government thought it was best.
But who am I to say
If their decision was wrong or right.

In times before my great grandmother Catherine
Left, and fell in love in the West End of Bofin.
She helped make your descendants live on
And remember their heritage in poem and song.

Shark, your people tried to stay and live on you
Until they had no more to give.
When they left they cried and cried
But in their hearts they never said goodbye.

For even yet their spirits wake each morning to greet the sky.
They walk your fields
And dwell in peace as they watch
The sea and world pass by.

An Island Wake

Margaret Duffy, Inis Fraoigh

I had planned a full day's work and decided to start the day with a good breakfast. The toast was ready and the bacon sizzling nicely under the grill, when 'puff' the flame went out. "Oh great", I exclaimed. The gas cylinder was empty and the full one was still at the pier. I wanted my breakfast! No alternative, I'd have to fetch it. So, picking up the wheelbarrow in the garden, I set out for the pier. Approaching Barney's house, now derelict, I noticed a cow lying on her side. Her body looked rigid and her legs stretched straight out. With some feeling of unease I left the wheelbarrow and tentatively crept towards her. She was dead.

Breakfast forgotten, I grabbed the wheelbarrow and hurried back to the house. I knew the cow belonged to John Mór on Aranmore Island, so I telephoned the sad news. Later, I saw a punt leaving Aran and steering towards the strand below my house. Six men landed at the beach armed with spades. Working together, they buried the cow. The next morning in the back garden, as I was hanging towels out to dry, the air suddenly became electric. The earth beneath my feet trembled and the once serene, quiet morning filled with thundering noise. I thought, " Now, if I were in the Wild West, I would call this a stampede". Running quickly to the front garden, I couldn't believe my eyes, it *was* a stampede!

Around thirty to forty cows, led by the enormous white Charollais bull, were galloping, at full speed from the pier towards Barney's. The noise was deafening. The bull was roaring. The cows were bellowing and calling. Suddenly, answering calls came through the morning air from all parts of the island. Cows, and little calves trying to keep up, were running as fast as they could to join them. Pregnant mothers galloped in an ungainly fashion over the rough terrain. As they thundered past, I was glad to be safely fenced in, in my garden.

Excitedly, I telephoned my neighbours. "Come quickly, something strange is happening. Something you'll never see in your life again." They did and we watched the amazing drama unfold.

Led by the bull, they all converged on the newly dug grave of the dead cow. The bull standing alone on the grave roared and pounded his feet into the ground. Heads together and pointing towards the bull, the cows formed a ring around the grave. All the time, they pounded the ground with their feet, keened and called and the other animals. My neighbour Angela said "They're grieving. It's a wake".

The circle of cows was packed tightly together. Little calves tried frantically, in vain, to join the ring.

The amazing ritual, which lasted thirty minutes suddenly stopped. Four of five cows, standing on the grave, continued for a few minutes, and then all quietly dispersed in small groups. They departed with dignity, as humans would leave a funeral service and walked solemnly down to the strand. There they all sat unmoving and silent for three hours until the tide came in.

During this time, I made my way, respectfully and unseen by them, to view the grave. In the grass a perfect little circle of sand had been formed.

It was a privilege to have shared and witnessed this impressive event. The feelings of awe, respect and admiration remain.

Hurricane Lily
Miriam Dunne, Sherkin Island

A low wind moans and gusts about the house
A hint of what's to come.
Everything's in
Moved to a safe place or tied down,
A Force twelve they say
Never, she prays
But remembers what the ferryman said
With a look of glee about Hurricane Lily.

She lies awake till three but nothing comes.
It must have missed us, she thinks, relieved
But sleeps with earplugs just in case.
A savage world awakes her.
The house trembles, windows shake,
The garden lashed into a mad dance
It's trees turned black and stripped of leaves
And the sea a wild thing that roars and spews out foam
That flies about like snow.
Tossed baulks of wood and seaweed jumbled up
With tyres, plastic bottles, nets and ropes
And runaway buoys all stretched across the strand
A crazy palisade six feet tall.

Imagine slithering about trying to clear that up,
She thinks as the cat whirls through the door with a wail.
The lights flicker and a voice on the radio says
It'll blow itself out.
She imagines it doubling back and blowing itself away
Until all is quiet
And then, a pet day
With sun shining through windows thick with salt
And beyond, blue skies and peachy clouds
And streams that trickle gently round the house
As if to make up and atone.

First-Time Buyers
Miriam Dunne, Sherkin Island

Sometimes things turn out best when they're not planned, like falling in love or having children – or even finding your dream house. Having been through the first two I wasn't even thinking about the last, when one spring morning in London, without warning, I was hit by a wave of homesickness.

A sweltering flat in 60's Soho was no place to be in the summer with a one-year-old and Syd, who wanted to write in peace. Of course it wasn't only that. Ireland, the irresistible old sow, was calling me back. Not the Ireland I'd come from – Dublin with its familiar faces, friendly pubs and promise of success if you stood still long enough. No the other Ireland, the one that exists in the mind's eye when you've been away too long. Wild, desolate, eternal, impossible...

We put an ad in *The Irish Times*. "House wanted by the sea, cheap." The one reply we got was enough. It came from a Mrs. Carew O'Driscoll, who was offering a house on an island off the coast. It overlooked a sandy beach and had started life as a ballroom until the bishop closed it down because couples kept disappearing off into the sand dunes. The rent was seven pounds a month and it was free until July. After that we'd have to take potluck but Mrs. Carew O'Driscoll assured us, there were plenty of other houses going.

We packed in our well-paid jobs with the usual alibis – sudden death or disablement in the family back home, crammed everything we owned into four teachests and left.

The journey took a day and a half. As the bus pulled away, leaving us and our possessions on a quiet pier in west Cork, a boatman in a peaked cap summed us up at a glance.

"You're staying a while. There's time for a drink so."

Over a pint he introduced himself as John Willie and told us how he'd got the job. The ferryman before him had caught this terrible chill he couldn't shake off so he'd stripped naked in front of a roaring fire and rubbed himself down with whiskey, taking a slug now and then.

"But didn't he get too close to the fire," said John Willie solemnly, "and next minute went up in flames." He erupted into a fit of laughter and grew serious again. "Wasn't that a terrible thing?"

A few pints later he took us across. A small knot of people had gathered to meet the ferry.

"That must be the wife," I heard someone whisper as Syd carried the child ashore. I couldn't see how Syd, at six foot three, could ever be mistaken for a woman but then the 1960s, with long hair, frilly shirts and beads hadn't arrived in Ireland yet.

We settled quickly into the rhythm of the island. Like everyone else's, our lives were dictated by the weather. When it got too relentless you took to your bed and waited for it to pass. The pub never closed. Even when the publican went to the mainland he left pencil and paper on the counter so you could write down what you'd had. There was always too much money in the till when he came back as no one liked putting their hand in for change.

The time flew. It was nearly the end of June when we discovered there were no houses going. Everything was booked solid. We were in despair until Syd met an old woman along the road one day and helped her home with her bags.

"I hear you're looking for a house," she said. "I've one might suit you."

We couldn't find it at first. The road petered off into marshy bogland and gorse. We clambered over stone walls, and across prickly fields until, suddenly, the house appeared, tucked away at the bottom of a long valley, an old, stone building sitting on top of the ocean, the last house on the island. We had to hack our way to the front door. There was no sign of water or electricity and, when I looked in the window I nearly wept. The floor was made with beach pebbles hammered into the earth, orange boxes for furniture and a great black hole of a fireplace. It's impossible, I thought. We can't stay here. But it was either that or take the boat back to England. The only consolation was that the rent couldn't amount to much.

"How did it suit you?" Asked the woman shyly when we called in on the way back. Her name was Cissie and, over a boiled egg, she explained that she and her brother had given up the old house when neither of them could manage the walk. They never stopped thinking about it though, and her brother, who was failing, vowed he'd pay one last visit before he died.

"So now," she said after we'd eaten, "maybe you'd care to make me an offer."

We suggested five pounds a month.

"Ah no," said Cissie politely, "you're mistaking me. I mean for you to buy the place."

Syd and I looked at each other. We hadn't a penny. We had barely enough to last the summer and pay the fares back. As we wondered what impossible sum she had in mind, Cissie explained that her brother was falling away. Planting potatoes one week and pulling them up the next. He'd never see another winter. She wouldn't be far behind him and what would happen to the old house then?´

"The roof will fall in, the cattle lay waste and that will be the end of it." she went on. "I'd rest easier thinking of a young family to take care of it and not see it fall to ruin."

We told her we'd love to but couldn't afford to buy.

"Surely you could manage something," said Cissie.

'At the moment," said Syd, 'I'd be lucky to find even fifty pounds."

"Seventy," said Cissie.

"Sixty-five," suggested Syd.

And on that we settled it. When we went on to the pub to celebrate, the news had arrived before us.

"Sixty-five?" said John Willie. "You were robbed, the pair of you. You could have had it for fifty."

"And come winter you'll be washed out of your beds," piped up his companion.

Cissie's brother never did see another winter. He died a few weeks later, the day before we moved in. Between a howling gale, the flickering candles and his promise to pay a final visit, we didn't sleep a wink, expecting him to float in the door any minute.

Cissie wasn't far behind him. Towards the end she seemed to take a turn against us, passing on the road without a greeting or closing her door when we came by. Then, suddenly she was as friendly as before. We were puzzled until John Willie explained that some young divil had climbed up on her roof one night and called down the chimney:

"Cissie, Cissie, it's your brother calling. I'm up here in Heaven but I can't rest easy thinking of our old house and how you let it pass to strangers." John Willie roared with laughter and added quickly: "But don't worry. I gave him a good talking to. And herself, too, for such foolishness."

By now, Cissie and her brother are resting easy. Remembering how it was when we first moved in, I think we've taken good care of it. So far, touch wood, we haven't been washed out of our beds although once or twice the Atlantic has come knocking at our door. And, after forty odd years on Sherkin, we're no longer strangers.

Waiting

Joanne Elliot, Inisbofin

For as long as I can remember, the photograph stood in on top of the piano in my mother's front room. It wasn't a very clear photograph being more brown and cream than black and white and slightly fuzzy around the edges, but the subjects were recognisable. My mother was in the centre, her short dark hair cut angularly around her high cheekbones. The other two were slender girls whose long fair hair was held by satin ribbons like Alice in Wonderland. They were dressed alike in white muslin, my mother though, had hiked hers up with a sash to give it a shorter, more fashionable look. The three were looking into the camera smiling, their arms around each other's waists, their studied pose showing nothing of the gulf which separated the Misses O'Toole from the pretty daughter of the village drunk.

That gulf widened into a chasm when my mother forgot herself long enough to marry an itinerant labourer who wandered into the village one day, a spade carried across his shoulders and a Bible in his hip pocket. A Protestant Bible. Even though Mam did her duty, even though she and her children were the first into Mass every Sunday and Holy Day, even though her fingers stitched the finest alter cloths that St. Colm's Church ever possessed, the village of Dunglas would never forget or forgive the terrible transgression on the part of one who was born into the true religion.

A year almost to the day of that shocking wedding, the disgrace was compounded. My mother's only brother, my uncle Sean, shook the mud of Dunglas from his boots, made his way to the 'Black North' and into the recruiting offices of the British Army.

When peace came, uncle Sean was in Canada, an aircraft technician with a marketable skill. Communications with him were limited to a card at Christmas written by his wife and enclosing a snapshot of their family, generally standing in front of a house which got increasingly larger and more elaborate.

The Misses O'Toole, meanwhile inured in their position as the most important family in Dunglas, population 212, continued to serve in their father's pub and shop, waiting for himself to find them the husbands who would come up to the O'Toole standards.

Suitable suitors were scarce on the ground in Connemara though. The big estates that had housed the gentry for hundreds of years had been broken up by land reform and taxes. The few that remained were owned mainly by English bohemian types, certainly not eligible for Miss Maggie or Miss Nora O'Toole. The sons of the well-to do either went into the Church or left for Galway or Dublin. The O'Toole girls had little education, no particular talents and had never travelled more than fifty miles from home. The Princes Charming were not knocking on the doors of O'Toole's Bar.

The late 40's brought a glimmer of prosperity. A new grocery shop opened in the village which sold tinned fruit, sliced bread, corn flakes and other new fangled stuff which Captain O'Toole refused to dispense in the ill lighted shop which had served for generations as the focal point of Dunglas life. Even his supply of sweets became increasingly stale and fly spotted.

Miss Nora who had kept the floor swept and the hearth piled with turf, now languished in bed most of the day. Her girth increased as her prospects dwindled and soon illness, at first imagined and even longed for, became reality. Miss Maggie struggled alone to serve the customers, wait on her evil tempered father, and fulfil the needs of her whey faced sister whose complaints mewed far into the night. She grew thin as Nora grew fat, her arms sinewy, her body stringy with undesired flesh.

I passed the pub every day on my way to school, its heavy wooden door shuttered against the morning. By afternoon the Captain was usually resting his rheumatic arms on the counter, scowling at the village youngsters who scurried quickly past the open door. Women never crossed the threshold once the sun was down except for Maura Burke who was up to no good. The local men though, went in every night, even the young lads. It was a place to keep dry and to escape from the tedium of sitting in the family kitchen watching Mam darn the socks.

In the 50's, I was struggling with exams at the convent school to which I had won a scholarship, the islands off the coast began to be developed as holiday resorts. The fortunes of Dunglas improved when the off-shore ferry docked at its wharf. My father seized the opportunity to open a shop selling oilskins, Wellington boots, camping supplies, sun glasses and postcards to the tourists. My mother, not to be outdone in initiative, hung out a B&B sign intent on catching the visitors from the islands.

In the 60's boom, any place connected with the tourist trade flourished and my parents were even able to take package holidays to Spain in the winter. I qualified as a teacher, then married a medical student. In time we were comfortably ensconced in a detached house in Galway complete with central heating, wall-to-wall carpeting and two bathrooms. I rarely visited Dunglas. It seemed easier for my parents to visit me where they enjoyed the cinema, the shops and 'our son-in-law, the doctor'. My father's religion, to which he stubbornly clung despite all attempts to convert him, ceased to be a liability as the Irish struggled to disengage themselves from Mother Church.

Throughout this period, however, the big square house at the end of Dunglas pier remained unchanged. Miss Maggie weighted down by the Captain's iron fist, came and went, thinner and more gaunt than ever. Miss Nora hardly appeared except for the times when she was taken by ambulance to the various hospitals and nursing homes where she was treated for her wasted life.

With the arrival of my third child, came great excitement. Uncle Sean came to visit my parents, a smooth prosperous stranger with a North American twang. One afternoon, he called to the hospital with a large bouquet of flowers for me and a silver christening cup for the baby.

We were walking back to my room from a visit to the nursery window when I caught sight of Nora O'Toole, shuffling along the corridor in a soiled pink dressing gown, her pendulous breasts in the thin cotton nightie, only half covered. She held a magazine in one hand.

"Hello," I said, "how are you Miss Nora?"

I could feel my uncle, who was holding my arm, stiffen. The old woman looked up, her vacant eyes blinking a little in surprise.

"Oh, so it's you, Mary Catherine," she whispered. "You're well, I hope".

"Quite well," I replied. "I've just had a baby girl. You remember my uncle Sean."

Miss Nora shifted her glaze to the figure on my left. Slowly, a deep flush rose from her flabby neck and suffused her pudding-like face. The magazine in her hand began to flutter. Then she blanched and fell heavily in a heap at our feet.

I shot down the corridor to summon a nurse. When we returned, Miss Nora was sitting on the floor, leaning against the wall. Uncle Sean was kneeling beside her, holding her hands. She was weeping hysterically and my uncle's eyes were suspiciously moist. He helped the nurse to lift her into a wheelchair and then, still holding the fat, white hand, accompanied them down the corridor.

I went back to my room and Uncle Sean appeared after a while. He sat down in an armchair beside the window and began to murmur.

"She was so lovely, Catherine. You've no idea how pretty she was then, so fresh and young. We were all young then, of course, and it was a lovely summer that year, balmy and mild. We'd been to a dance out on one of the islands, a whole crowd of lads and girls from the village. St. John's Night it was. We lit a bonfire on the beach. But a sea swell had come up and the boats couldn't get back so we had to stay all night on the island, the girls in one house, the lads in another. Nothing improper in it. In those days, if you so much as held a girl's hand, you were engaged, or should be. It was almost noon the next day when we landed back at Dunglas. We were all laughin' and singin', still drunk from the night before, not with porter, mind you, just high spirits. Nora and I were planning to be married but she hadn't told her Da yet. He was a fierce one as ye well know." He paused for a moment and I reflected on how quickly his voice had regained the cadence of his youthful speech.

"As the curragh came up to the wharf at Dunglas, I could see old man O'Toole, hurrying down the quay from the shop, his face as dark as the blackthorn stick in his hand. By the time he reached us, the girls were already climbing the ladder. I gave them a hand up and I could feel Nora tremble when she saw himself.

'I'm sorry, Da,' she whipered. 'We couldn't help it. The boat couldn't go...' 'Get ya home,' he snarled. 'You and your sister. I'll deal with ye later.' Then he turned to me, thrust his beaky nose into my face and roared like a madman. 'If I ever catch the likes of ye lifting yer dirty eyes to my girls, I'll flay ye alive!' I don't know how I got the courage, but I managed to squeak, 'I love Nora. I want to marry her.'

'Marry her?' he screamed. 'Ye, the son of a layabout. Ye, with a black Protestant for a brother-in-law! Marry an O'Toole? Ye aren't fit to clean our boots!'

Then he swung his stick at me and cracked me across the head. I tried to duck the next blow, lost my balance and fell. He pulled back his leg, gave me a gigantic kick and I went over the edge of the wharf into the sea. The bastard never even waited to see if I could swim. He stalked up the quay and I could hear the pub door bang shut even though I was in the water a hundred yards away."

"What did you do?"

"I waited 'till Sunday. I knew that O'Toole hurried home after Mass to open the bar leaving Nora and Maggie to walk back alone. I stopped them in the road. Nora tried to hurry past me, Maggie urging her on. They were terrified that someone might tell the Da. I begged Nora to run away with me. We could go to Dublin. With the war there was plenty of work in the cities. I was willing to do anything. I'd never let her want. But she was too frightened. I thought Maggie might talk sense to her but she had been brainwashed too. Thought Nora deserved better than a village lad with a drunken father and a sister who was married to a Protestant.

I couldn't bear to stay in Dunglas after that so I went to war. I've never been back until this week. Never knew what happened to her."

His voice broke and his fumbled for a packet of cigarettes in his pocket.

"I think she waited," I said, after a while. "For you to come back. For him to die. For her life to begin. She's waiting still."

"I suppose so," he said, lighting up. "I suppose so."

Deora Saillte

Máirín Uí Fhearraigh, Oileán Ghabhla

Bhí maidin bhreá ann, an mhaidin úd i ndeireadh Lúnasa na bliana 1967. Bhí leoithne bheaga gaoithe ag séideadh ó dheas agus bhí an fharraige rud beag clabach. Ní raibh mórán fonn ormsa éirí. Níor chodail mé néal i rith na hoíche agus b'fhada mé ag urnaí nach dtiocfadh an lá seo go deo, ach caithfidh sé nár chuala Dia mé. Bhí an teach lán daoine agus bhí siad uilig gnóthach. Ní raibh mise amuigh as an leaba mar a ba cheart go raibh beirt de na comharsana ar shiúil amach an doras agus mo leaba leo. I ndiaidh greim bricfeasta, d'iarr mo mháthair orm aire a thabhairt do na hainmhithe. Ní raibh sin doiligh a dhéanamh mar go dtug Johnaí Tom, an búistéir as Machaire Chlochair, leis an bhó bhuí, an bhó bhreac agus an bearach an lá roimh ré agus ní raibh fágtha anois ach an t-asal, cúpla cearc, dhá lacha agus bardal.

Ní raibh a fhios agam féin caide a bhí ag tarlú mar níor inis aon duine a dhath dom ach go mbeinn ag dul go scoil úr ar an Luan mar gur druideadh an scoil s'againne agus gurbh éigean don mháistreás imeacht.

Bhí an t-éadach uilig pacáilte ag mó mháthair le cúpla lá agus cuireadh an trunca mór donn isteach ar an charr i gcuideachta na cathaoireach móire ina suíodh mo mháthair mhór i gcónaí cois na tine. Bhí an t-asal agus an carr aníos agus síos go Port an Chruinn i rith na maidine go dtí nach raibh áit suí ná luí sa teach.

Chruinnigh na comharsana isteach ansin agus thosaigh an caoineadh. Bhí mise ag caoineadh fosta ach ní raibh a fhios agam cad chuige.

Chuaigh mo mháthair suas go hArd an mBáinseog agus shuigh sí ar 'an chloch,' cloch mhór liath ar thaobh Ard an mBáinseog a raibh radharc ar an oileán uilig uaithi. Bhí sí ansin tamall fada ach níor ligeadh domsa dul suas chuici.

Tháinig sí anuas i gcionn tamaill fhada agus dúirt sí: 'Seo, bhuel, rachaidh muid chun bealaigh le cuidiú Dé' agus shiúil sí amach an doras agus níor amharc sí ar ais ní ba mhó. Shiúil mná an bhaile síos go dtí an ché linn áit a raibh bád an teaghlaigh, 'Nancy' ag fanacht le muid a thabhairt amach go tír mór. Bhí an bád lán agus cuireadh mise i mo shuí ar an trunca mór donn thiar chun deiridh.

Bhí m'uncail, Neidí Jimí Mac Suibhne ar an inneall, na comharsana, Hughie Hiúdaí Shíle Ó Rabhartaigh ar an stiúir agus scaoil Johnaí Mhicí Ruaidh Ó Domhnaill na rópaí agus d'fhág muidinne Gabhla, an baile ina rugadh agus tógadh muid agus thug muid ár n-aghaidh ar shaol úr.

Gabhla

Maírín Uí Fhearraigh, Oileán Ghabhla

Tá na bádaí ar feistiú
Ag cé Phort an Chruinn,
Tá an toit ag éirí,
Go hard sa spéir.

Tá an t-eallach ag géimneach,
thall ar an Ard Breac,
tá na héanacha go ceolmhar,
amuigh ag an Loch.

Tá an t-uisce ag slioarnaigh,
thart fan Tór Glas,
agus is fairsing an chreathnach,
thíos ar an leac.

Tá na fir ag comhrá,
Ar Mhullach ar Aird,
Agus na páistí ag scairtigh,
Thíos ag an scoil.

Tá asal agus carr,
Amuigh ar Chnoc a Chait,
Tá fir ag togáil na móna,
Atá chomh dubh leis an bhac.

Tá mná an bhaile,
Gnóthach fad,
Iad ag bácáil is ag níochán,
is ag maistriú go ceart.

I mo chuimhne, sin Gabhla,
Lá breá Samhraidh, fadó.

Oileán Ghabhla Inné agus Inniu

Síle Nic Aodh Uí Ghallchóir, Oileán Ghabla

Oileán mo shinsear,
Mo Mhamaí ar ndóigh,
Lán craic agus gleo,
Scoth na bhfear le urraú,
Le heolas na mara,
Ní féidir a shárú.

Oileán beag seasca,
Bhfuil loch ann le heascainn,
Tréan sloag agus crainnigh,
Crubaigí agus bairnigh.

Ann aimsir na scadán,
Bhí na bádaí ar seol,
Ann séasúr na mbradán,
Bhí na gasúir ag ceol.

Ann seasca seacht,
Druideadh an scoil,
B'éigean do mhuintir Ghabhla,
Bogadh go tír mór,
In éadan a dtoil.

B'shin tús leis an deireadh,
Tréigeadh Gabhla,
Gan criostaí,
Agus a sheal tugtha.

Ach anois ar na mallaibh,
Tháinig páistí 67 le fuinneamh,
Agus tá pleananna go leor acu,
Do Ghabhla agus don todhchaí.

Maireann an muintearas,
An suáilceas is an cairdeas,
Ó ghlúin go glúin,
Oidhreacht luachmhar an teaghlaigh.

Muna bhfuil mise meallta,
Tá saol úr dúinn geallta,
Agus beidh leictreachas is gleo,
Fá chladaí fá bhallaí,
I nGabhla go deo.

Smaointe Oileán
Síle Nic Aodh Uí Ghallchóir, Oileán Ghabla

Ó thús an tsaoil sheas mé go maorga,
Sínte siar ó chósta Thír Chonaill,
Ó thuaidh uaim tá Gaoth Dobhair, siar tá na Rossa,
Ar mó chúl tá Meiriceá agus na mílte farraigí móra,
'S cé chreidfeadh an t-am úd go gcaillfinnse mo ghlóire.

Bhí agam uair amháin teaghlach beo bríomhar,
Dream a bhí gealgháireach, glórach agus gníomhach,
Ach ag tús na seascaidí tháinig scaipeadh 's sceoin,
Ar mo theaghlach beag seascair a bhog go tír mór,
Duine ar dhuine i gcoinne a dtola,
Bánaíodh mo chroich sa siocair druid na scoile.

Ó thús mo shaoil chuir mé cothú ar fáil,
Do mo chlann groí a bhí fearúil 's fíor,
Le raidhse bídh a bhí folláin don chroí,
Toradh na talún agus flaithiúlacht na farraige,
Le meitheal i ngach páirc,
Le criú i ngach Bád,
Chruthaigh mo phobal saol an toicí.

Chuaigh mo thoibheach i ndise, níl dear le fáil,
Chuaigh mo pháirceanna ar fiáin, gan prátaí, gan cál,
Níl claí nó fál ina seasamh go buan,
Le cur i mo chuimhne an dream a d'imigh uaim.

Beidh a cuid féin ag an fharraige agus is fíor é le rá,
Chaill mise clann ionúin 's iad i mbéal trá,
Ar an 4ú Feabhra sa bhliain 43,
Ghoid sí go fealltach uaim Éamonn Bán 's a chriú,
Ach deirim go fóill mo thoil le toil Dé,
'S guím beannacht na bhflaitheas ar a n-anam geal glé.

Thréig mo chlann mé 's clann mo chlainne,
Fágadh liom féin mé íseal gan fuinneamh,
Blianta fada, ag feitheamh, ag fanacht go fíor,
Le casadh na taoide, le fíoradh na físe,
Go bpilleadh mo pháistí roimh dheireadh na mílaoise.

Ach anois is muid in aois seo ar dTiarna 2004,
30 bliain is corradh ó leagadh an chloch dheiridh ar mo leacht,
Phill clann Nellie Jimmy ag ath-thógáil a dtí,
's chuir siad go déanach ionamsa athnuachan 's brí

Inniu, mothaím arís mar Rí ar mo chine,
Tá mo theaghlach ag pilleadh duine ar dhuine,
Tá soilse á lasadh, tá comhrá fá thithe,
Tá na bóithre mín, tá tithe á dtógáil,
Tá saol nua sroite 's tá maolú ar m'uaigneas,
Milte altú do Dhia as ucht an tsuáilcis,
Gura fada buan a mhaireas mé,
Mar tá mise Oileán Ghabhla ar ais i mbarr mo réime.

M'Oileánaigh
Olwen Gill, Inis Mór

Shiúil mé ag súil
Lá cois trá
Agus rith sé liom
Go rithfidh sé liom
Nó sí,
Amach anseo.

Beidh dúnta 's ailltreacha
An oileáin fúinn
Tuile 's trá na taoille,
Beidh gaoithe
Gaineamh, gréine,
Éanlaith, blátha, daoine
An chloch aoil álainn
Mar eachtra againn
Amach anseo.

Agus bhí.

Shiúil muid
Sheoil muid
Shnámh muid,
D'fháilte muid
Catachánín beag rua
Mar dheirfiúrín
'S deartháirín beoga bricíneach
'S d'fhiosraigh siad, d'eachtraigh siad
'S neartaigh siad triúr
Faoi shaibhreas inse.

Ritheann siad anois
Ar fud an domhain mhóir
Agus mo bhuíochas don oileán
A chothaigh iad.

Gone Fishing
Olwen Gill, Inis Mór

Had Nell learnt to say 'fuck off' earlier in life, she might now be able to enjoy a lie-in in her own home. At 67, with no bookings for the night, she still felt guilty for heading off for a walk before anyone from the morning boat could arrive looking for a room. The house would be empty for the first time in months if she hurried. "Sorry, we're full" was not an option for Nell, she would feel lousy sending them a further mile up the road to the next B&B when they had already braved the mile with bags, to her house from the pier. If she were not there, she could not be held responsible so she had better get her skates on.

The phone rang; a chatty American who could not believe how clear the line was, thinking about making arrangements for next summer. Nell listened to his family tree, his hopes and aspirations for his forthcoming expedition keeping an eye on the clock. "Do you drink Guinness, I love Guinness? Do you have television? Are there any cars there, how did they get there? Is it wild in winter? Are there any O'Mahoneys living there, maybe we're related?" Nell eventually assured him that when he had exact dates, he would have no problem securing a room for next summer in six months time. What she should have said was, "Sorry, I won't be in business this time next year", or possibly use the F word but what she did say was, "thank you for calling and I'll be looking forward to meeting you soon."

It was late August, the time when Nell secretly swore that this would definitely be her last summer taking in guests. There was a few bob in the box and the enthusiasm for the first few visitors of the season had long since waned to a perfunctory rattling off of meal times, boat times, bus times, names of the pubs with music and a finger point in the general direction of Dún Aonghusa.

When Nell finally got off the phone, she opened the door to a few hours of freedom and fresh air only to find a very young couple locked in embrace on her doorstep. They giggled as they disengaged and he explained that they were newlyweds. "Only yesterday", beaming proudly. An unusual looking couple, children rather than adults. Her hair totally covered by a bright scarlet scarf, pinned somehow under her neck but still flowing down over her young frame. She gazed lovingly at her man-child as he spoke to Nell about their needs and budget. He had a little Irish and was delighted to use it. His new bride did not speak English, she had just moved to Ireland but he was proud to interpret and decipher on her behalf.

Nell plastered on her "céad mile fáilte" as best she could, knowing that it was as easy to let them in as to spend the time making alternative arrangements, in sign language with the bride or in very limited book Irish with the groom. She did answer his "Cé méid airgead do leaba agus bricfeasta?" slowly and distinctly but felt like adding "agus tá sé a wallop with a white wash brush!"

She showed them their room, gave them a key and would leave a tray of tea things in the sitting room; they could then come and go as they pleased. The groom seemed to have a bit of difficulty figuring out if the bride knew what a tray of tea was or indeed if she ever touched the stuff. He did not seem to know if she took coffee either! Wondering how the hell they managed to communicate and get to know one and other, much less marry, Nell locked up her own side of the house and headed off at last, out into the salty air and sunshine.

Her route was as beautiful and intoxicating as ever. The sea, the cliffs, the flowers, the birds, all conspired to lift her spirits. Tired limbs soon began to relax and with each delight she came upon, a rabbit, an orchid, the splash of a wave, Nell's gait and humour lifted. When she finally walked towards home, the resentment towards her lodgers had all but disappeared although she still hoped that they would be gone off to see the sights sparing her a question and answer session.

Nell went to clear the tea things but found them all untouched. The full tea pot gone cold, the cups still upside down on saucers, scones butter and jam as she left them, but all was not right. There was a smell, a strange scent which filled and itched her nostrils. Not a bad smell but strong and different nonetheless. Opening the door to the corridor lined with bedrooms and bathrooms, she was washed over by a wave of steam and smothered in a perfumey mist.

Nell thought of fire or flood or both and had fifty flash thoughts of how to deal with it as she headed at speed through the corridor. She stopped in the steamy haze on a soggy floor outside the far bathroom, her nostrils twitching from the citrussy, overpowering though still not totally unpleasant smell, which had replaced the normal sea air, and cleaning fluids. She reached for the door handle, it was slimy with orange goo, the door was dripping wet on the outside, she was about to push it open when it dawned on her that she was now discovering how the newly weds were getting to know one and other – their means of communication. Whooshing and splashing, laughing and loving loudly behind her bathroom door and previously all around her house if the steam and puddles were anything to go by, language was obviously not an issue!

Squelching, she retreated back to her own side of the house, half pleased for them, half mortified and a bit annoyed. She had gone along with the improvements of "hot & cold" sinks and central heating in all the rooms but had balked at the latest trend of "ensuites" not simply because of the cost but because of the further commitment that it would entail. She may have been wrong on that one and thanked the Lord that there were no other guests. What would the Sisters of last week have made of this interruption to their rosary, or the twelve-year-old twin boys that had left that very morning had they needed an afternoon pee? Her regulars, the elderly Misses Shaw Smiths would certainly not have remained silent had they been staying.

Nell stayed well out of earshot until next morning when she had no option but to make small, very small talk as she served them breakfast. They held hands and mauled one another whilst she answered his "Conas a tá tú ar maidin?" with a very civil " Go maith" instead of the "more rested than you" that she would like to have thrown back at him.

They left after two further long days and nights of seriously getting to know one another, if the volume from behind the bathroom door was anything to go by! Cleaning up when they left, Nell came across two large empty plastic bottles of massage oil in the bin in the far bathroom, very obviously the source of the citrus scent. Nell opened every window in the house and stripped all the beds, she knew that this was it; this would actually be her very last season. She was claiming her house back. She turned the radio up to full volume and felt the vibration in the floorboards. If other people could enjoy her home at all times of the day and night then why the hell shouldn't she? She would go to Galway on the morning's boat and pay a visit to all the booking offices and have them remove her B&B from their lists. She would buy a decent supply of fishing tackle and then she just might call into the cosmetics counter in 'Moons' for a few bottles of Exotic Orange Blossom bath and massage oil on her way home!

An Oíche Sin

Thomond Gill, Inis Mór

Ghoid tú an domhan
Le do shúile donn
An oíche sin

B'fhuath liom thú
Fad a bhí tú ag tnúth
Leis an oíche sin

B'fhearr liom bás
Ná tú a bheith ag fás
Roimh an oíche sin

Nuair a thóg mé do lámh
Agus thit mé i ngrá
Leat an oíche sin

Housework
Thomond Gill, Inis Mór

She cried a river
When she left you.
I washed the dishes
in her tears.

I shined the glasses,
with the warm from
your imagined breath
ringing softly in her ears.

I fluffed the pillows
with her sobs
and hung the sheets
to dry. Her tears

Did not stop as
I mopped the floor
on which she stood
Still. Not sure. Those years.

I made the bed
and laid her down,
and in that crisp new night,
I gathered tears.

I boiled them up
with camomile, to calm her.
then poured them in a cup
and made her drink.

She tossed and turned
that night. She left you.
I wrote this poem
to the sound of her tears,

Then lay so still.
She left you, that night,
her face was wet with tears.
And I? I too have fears.

If I Would Have Taken Ten Photos....
Thomond Gill, Inis Mór

I'd have shot the laughing girl in the ragged, still shiny, wheelchair
manoeuvring the crowded biscuit aisles in Supervalu
and blown her up so you could see her too bright white eye,
Jaffa cakes. And dirty pink Converse.

I'd have framed the feeling on the girl in the pinstripe suit's face
Walking along the busy sunny morning quays
And focused on the way in trees sunny green light lie
the secrets to A happy universe.

I'd have captured the confused look about the blonde pig-tailed girl
Holding her fat sisters hand that didn't hold back
And zoomed in on her crooked grey skirt and school tie,
Striped. Her shirt and innocence.

I'd have blurred the faces of those who hurried past
The dirty man who sat on Grafton St.
And in the foreground shown his black brown yellow feet
Blistered, unmoving as he rocked.

I'd have snapped the Chinese man who pushed a pram
And laughed and talked to his spiky haired son
In a wideshot that showed the bank and the cars
And how empty that shadowy backstreet is.

I'd have a close-up of my roommate on the couch
Snuggled in a blanket cos she's sick
A mise en scene of toilet roll, Lemsip, blue blanket,
Remote control and Cornetto.

I'd have made a collage of the girl in the fluorescent orange boa
on the balcony at the party next door:
mixed media with a broken speaker, an alarm clock
showing 5.30am, Monday morning. And slept for a while.

The last three I would have taken of you…

That look on your face as you concentrated to undo my
necklace as you lay on me with no shirt on.
The way your long eyelashes lay on your cheeks as you slept
And how your eyes lit up when you saw me

But I will not capture your soul. I want it for my own.

The Ticket Collector
Thomond Gill, Inis Mór

He looks like a man who has travelled far,
    a white scar maps the journey,
it marks his dark face and darker past.
His limp draws questions: How? Why?
        What from? Did he run?
The scar meanders through his eye
(the crooked path that brought him here),
    through pink speckles on his cheek
        it continues down his neck,
        hidden by a shirt and tie,

    I do not know his destination.

Away from family, a land, a home.
    A transportation in transit.
        Trains. Tickets. Time
to notice all the things that I,
    who travels reading, do not:
    the marker that signals the end;
this tree; that field; those houses;
the little journeys people make, and more.
    Keeping his eye on the horizon
        he punches hard and smiles.

That Time in January
Thomond Gill, Inis Mór

I stood on the white sand,
higher up.
And watched as she played in the waves
of his clear blue eyes.
Dancing. Delighted. Laughing
off the cold that hit her,
now and then.
Blinded by the sun
she could not see
any deeper, but I did,
and stood by.
I let him take her.
I waited
as she waded
through her murky waters
and watched her emerging.
Bitter. Cold. And Blue.

Island Mist
Pauline Hanley, Bere Island

Walking, soft mist
Wrapping itself around me like an old fleece.
Caressing, comforting, ambivalent to its usefulness.
Not everyone's idea of style.

Climbing Murphy's height – breathless –
I am revived by the feathery caress of light rain.
Light as angels' breath – Silk on skin.
Not practical but beautiful in its impracticality.

Passing the gallán, aware of its presence,
Unaware of its true history.
It evades questioning, standing sentry over an island people,
Defined by its complexity.

Sheltered now on both sides – the wind rises,
Feeling smug for I am not within its reach.
I hear distant waves molding change
And pray for sameness.

Arriving at the crossroads. Turning left for home.
Taking the hill to the hotel as if in battle,
Pretence of reverie faded. Facing the wind. Mismatched forces.
Realising now

A soft mist can become a dangerous thing.

Bailéad an Phíolóta

(Fonn: She Moved Through the Fair)
Máire Uí Iarnáin, Inis Mór

I dtús na hathbhliana
Míle naoi gcéad ochtó naoi
Bhí crith talún is timpistí
Ag tarlú thoir agus thiar;
Bhí eitleáin á bpléascadh
Is fir sáinnithe faoi thith'
Ach ba mheasa linn thar aon ní
Bás phíolót' Thennessee.

Tháinig scéala ón tSionainn
Roimh cheathrú chun a naoi
Go raibh eitleán Piper
Ar a bhealach aniar;
Bhí an oíche siúd dorcha,
Ní raibh gála ann ná gaoth
Ach bhí tanc amháin folamh
Is gan aon ola ag dul tríd.

Chuaigh lasracha an Fraser[1]
In aer go breá buí;
Faoi cheann cúpla nóiméad
Bhí an t-ancaire aníos;
Bhí an criú ar bord loinge
Is iad feistithe chun gnímh,
Bhí chuile ní réitithe
Lena threorú i dtír.

---

1 Margaret Russell Fraser = An Bád Tarrthála

Scaoileadh téada báid iascaigh
Gan fuadar is gan flosc;
Ní raibh bus, carr ná leoraí
Nach raibh lasta ar Rinn Mhéith;
Tháinig an Piper go corrach
Aniar os a gcionn
Ach chuaigh sé ceann faoi sna maidhmeanna
Soir amach ó Phort Dae.

Is nárbh fhada an turas é
ó Thalamh an Éisc
Is tú ag taisteal id aonar
Go hard ins an spéir;
Bhí chuile chúnamh le fáil agat
Ar muir is ar tír,
Nár mhór an mí-ádh tú a dhul síos
gar d'Oileán na Naomh.

Go ndéana Dia grásta ar phíolóta
Mhemphis Tennessee
Is ar iascairí Árann
Nár fritheadh ariamh;
Nára fada uainn an Dauphin
Is soilse ar Rinn Mhéith
Le muid a shaorú ó chruatan
Is ó bhás anabaí.

Caitlín Maude
Máire Uí Iarnáin, Inis Mór

I gceartlár chroí na Rosa
I dtús an Fhómhair '91
Bhí scoth ban Éireann bailithe
I gcuimhne Chaitlín Mháidhbh,
Ógbhean fhuinniúil, chairdiúil
Banfhile agus ealaíontóir
A tógadh sa gceantar sin
Tar éis naoi déag is dhá scór.

Chuir sí suim sa bhfilíocht
Ó bhí sí fíor-óg;
Theann sí leis an drámaíocht
Is bhain amach an ghlóir;
An gheamaireacht ná an óráid
Níor chuir uirthi aon stró
Is go seasfá sa sneachta léi
Is í ag gabháil de Dhónall Óg.

Labhair sí An Ghaeilge go nádúrtha
ins gach áit dá ndeachaigh sí;
Ba í a bhunaigh "An Bonnán Buí"
A chuidigh le foghlaimeoirí.
D'oibrigh sí go dícheallach
Is chuir an gníomh i gcrích
Nuair a bhí scoil Ghaeilge le baint amach
Do pháistí Bhaile Átha Cliath.

Chonaic mise Caitlín uaim
I dtús na seachtódaí;
Bhí spreacadh agus fuinneamh
Sa bhfáidh bhí os mo chomhair.
Chuir sí rabharta cainte di
Go fíochmhar is go seoigh–
Mhol sí bunadh na Gaeltachta
Ár dteanga is ár meon
Is chuir fainic orainn ár gcultúr a choinneáil
Mar go dtiocfadh ann dó fós.

Bheinnse i mo thost anocht
Dá mbeadh Caitlín ar an saol;
Chuirfeadh sí an chluain oraibh
Le briathra binn' a béil;
Labhródh sí faoin bhfostaíocht
Faoin timpeallacht is faoi bhóithre Dhoire Né
Is ba é tús agus deireadh a paidre
Teilifís Ghaeltachta dúinn féin.

Mholfadh sí An Pléaráca
Atá á chruthú féin go tréan
Mar a mhol Clíona Cussen agus Máirtín,
File, a gcomhleacaí féin;
Mholfadh sí an dul chun cinn, an misneach
Atá ag roinnt lena muintir féin
Mar a mholaimse an comhluadar
Nach ligeann a cuimhne in éag.

Gráinnín Snaoise
Nóilín Ní Iarnáin, Inis Mór

Seanfhear maorga
Caipín speic[1]
Maide láimhe
Gráinnín snaoise.
Muirfhuílleach
Lonradh ar ghaineamh
Is ar fharraige;
An spéir ag bruth
Le teas na gréine;
Gasúir bheaga
Ag déanamh iontais
De ghráinnín snaoise.

---

1 Peaked cap

Scent of Memories
Catherine Lavelle, Inisbofin

Spring awakens with scents of musk
and ocean spray
of opened soil, budding shrubs
and stale bedroom air

The wise old man treads the daily path
along the brackish scrub
to the thatched barn that he calls a house
where he was born

The handle-less kettle from when he was a boy
boils on the hearth till quenched
tainted clothes seek comfort
from sea and sky

Summer brings the tossing of the hay
and the anger of the honey bees
the silhouette of endurance
glimpsed from Rusheen Bay

Back again across the sands at midnight
night-light of moon to guide his way
disquiet awaiting his footsteps, high tide, no torch
and a multitude of possibilities

Welcomes the cackling of incense
from the roaring fire
the ritual of filling the pipe, eyes fixed
on the shadows overhead

'Did you call into Maggie's on your way down?'
and "How is she?"
'Oh, grand, she has a fine fire
but the coal it has no smoke'

Heads lean together over the hearth
even his well-worn cap alights in the dark
he does this journey for forty years
until he can no longer cross the sands

Still stands proudly and secretly looking across
the bay with cataract eyes
at the thatch now leaking and boarded up
that was his home

Wasteland
Catherine Lavelle, Inisbofin

I am unique in my occupying space,
Ugly, nebulous and seemingly barren of a worthy place.
My fellow colonists taunt me with invection and scorn,
For fear of infiltrating their safe shields.

I do not want to be here,
Nor know of the origins of my co-existence,
But my ample strength surpasses my malformation.
My host writhes in rhythmic discharge,
Whooping sounds all around.

It's not my choice to play the dice,
Or sap the foundations of this languid life.
They try and breathe vengeance with magnetic waves,
And I find solace deeper in the tubular caves.

The Homecoming
Catherine Lavelle, Inisbofin

There you sit in childlike gesture
Your essence diminished
Your anger and plight palpable

Eleven days till your last agonies
And yet you have not reached a place of tranquillity
Pale anthers subdued by fear
The prey of a hungry claw awaiting pasture
'Do I look bad?' you keep asking
Between your speechless fright

People come and go
And you recall vivid memories and tales of past times
Such heightened awareness and lucidity of thought

Your last words
'Who will feed me when you leave?'
Surge the river's banks like an overfilled teacup

Childlike gestures slip away
To a sleep of raptured rest
You could be with us some time yet
A premature prey to grief

Island Roy
Julienne Loughlin, Island Roy

Wind – Rain
Music of the Isle
Distant waves
Dashing on Tramore
Deep silences
Velvet darkness
Enhancing
Mind and spirit
Unbroken awe
To gaze about
Salty seascape
Breadth of light
Island lovers
Joy – We shout.

Life Choice
Sabrina Verdecampo Mc Carron, Inis Mór

As the wind shook every window in the house and the rain poured down, Sam tried to remember all the reasons she had agreed to leave life in the city. It was times like these that made the island seem like the loneliest and most secluded place in the world. The harder the rain pounded down, the harder it was for Sam to concentrate.

She thought of the first day she had arrived on the island. It was a beautiful sunny day, the ferry glided over the calm waters as if gliding on ice. As they approached the pier, she could see beautifully painted houses, restaurants and pubs. She could only see a small portion of the island but already it intrigued her.

Sam smiled to herself thinking of her first encounter dealing with a small community. When the ferry approached the pier and her boyfriend, Mike, offered to carry her bags so that she could concentrate on walking off the gangway without tripping, she had asked who would possibly be paying attention to her as she walked off the ferry. He answered everyone! Sam had been so nervous she had wanted to throw up. She'd come from a town of forty thousand people and wasn't used to anyone caring about anything that didn't directly affect their own lives. At first she had thought everyone was very nosy. It was only after she had taken the time to get to know everyone that she realised that it wasn't nosiness at all that drove the locals' curiosity but an ability to sincerely care about everyone who visited their island. The people had been one of the major reasons she had decided to stay.

Sam sat in her sitting room staring out at the bucketing rain. Both her babies were fast asleep and she was taking advantage of a rare chance to relax and reflect. The second reason was harder to envision on a day like today. It had also hit her the day she arrived just in a more dramatic fashion. After a quick introduction to Mike's family and an even quicker bite to eat they had rushed out to the pub. There was a very important all-Ireland hurling match on. Sam couldn't follow the match but she loved watching the intensity of the people who could. Everyone acted as if every move the players made on the pitch directly affected each of them. Sam had never seen such passion. When the game ended and the team they were supporting won, the celebrating begun.

It was a few hours later when the sun had gone down and the moon and stars were shinning that Sam stepped out for a cigarette. She walked over to the wall overlooking the beach and the pier where she had arrived. She looked up at the sky and saw a million stars lighting it up. She hadn't even realised that so many stars existed. In the city, most nights you could nearly count the stars that you could see.

When the pub door fully closed leaving all of the chatter inside she heard something she had never heard in her life. It was the sound of complete and utter silence. There were no cars driving by, no buzzing of lamposts, even the water below her was completely still. At first, Sam was uncomfortable. She looked for anything to distract her from it, she fidgeted with her keys and rustled through her bag but once she allowed herself to feel it she began to enjoy it. An air of peacefulness swept over her. She stood there for what felt like hours being consumed by it. So deeply entranced by it that she hadn't noticed Mike's mother coming up behind her.

"You get used to it!" His mother said placing her hand on Sam's shoulder. Sam's skin leapt from the touch as it brought her back to where she was. "I hope not!" Sam answered. She never wanted to take this for granted. She never wanted this to just become the way it is. She hoped that the peacefulness always remained special.

Sam laughed now sitting on her sofa thinking to herself that after having had two babies peacefulness wasn't something that occurred often in her life anymore. Still, it was nice to know that it was there and obtainable when she really needed it.

The rain subsided and Sam decided to take the car and visit the third reason she had made the decision. Mike would mind the kids if they woke up. She drove to the shore. She watched the angry waves crash against each other and the seaside. They crashed so hard that foam was creeping up the rocks and onto the road. It was so thick it looked like snow. Some of it was floating in the air like tiny soap bubbles. The noise was like thunder breaking in the sky. Stormy days were always beautiful here.

Sitting in her car safely hidden from the storm, she thought of the first time Mike had taken her for a walk along the shore and up the cliffs. It had been a sunny day. They walked up along the cliffs that gradually rose to 300 feet like stairs to heaven. It felt like heaven to Sam, the view was breathtaking. At the top, Sam looked down and watched the water dance below them. It reminded her of a beautiful dance she had seen at a ceilí called the Siege of Ennis. The waves would line up to meet their partners exhaustingly twirling together until the rhythm changed and they would crash through to meet their next partner. It was beautifully orchestrated in a way that life could never be, each wave knowing their place and turn. The rhythm had swept over her as she watched and wondered how much fun it would be to be caught up in it all, though she would never dare.

The sound of the rain picking up again like little drummers on her windshield brought Sam back to the present. She started up the engine and drove home. As she parked in the driveway, she could see Mike in the sitting room playing with their two year old and holding the eight month old in his arms. All three of them were laughing.

Sam smiled to herself. The family they would rear together would grow up with the very rare chance these days of experiencing peacefulness, true beauty and a community full of people who sincerely cared about each other.

In The Hands of the Sea
Sabrina Verdecampo Mc Carron, Inis Mór

The alarm pierced through the cabin. Johnny was already awake feeling the ship roll from side to side. He jumped out of bed and got dressed; knowing that the alarm meant the storm had surpassed a force ten. All engineers were required on standby in the engine room. Almost out the door, he doubled back, grabbing the picture of his wife and eighteen month old son. He allowed himself a quick glance before slipping it into his pocket.

As he ran down the stairs, gripping the rail for support against the battering of the relentless waves, he remembered how he used to live for these storms. The North Atlantic run could be quite mundane after six months of back and forth from Canada to Europe. Crazy as it was, the winter provided a little bit of excitement. The storms promised winds and waves that would keep the officers and crew on their toes. The younger ones loved the rush of 45-degree rolls and 50 foot crashing waves, especially those without families at home waiting for them. Johnny had been one of those men, but all had changed for him the day Tommy was born. He no longer needed the excitement. These days, he was just happy making it home safely at the end of his contract.

He was two flights from the engine room when he saw the water running through the doorway from the A deck. He peeked his head into the hallway and saw the first mate yelling at the boson. The deck was flooded and at the end of the hallway the weather-tight door was left slightly ajar.

"Give me a hand, Johnny!" The first mate shouted.

"What happened here?" Johnny asked knowing he wouldn't like the answer.

"One of the AB's headed out on deck to secure the life rafts," Mitch explained.

"On whose orders? No one is allowed out on deck during a storm." Johnny questioned the boson.

"Not mine, sir. He went out on his own," replied the boson looking down at his feet.

Johnny felt sick knowing full well that no man would go out there unless they were ordered to yet he could be sure no one would ever find out what actually had happened. He silently cursed the unspoken oath they had all accepted to pledge: *What happens at sea, stays at sea.*

They struggled to push the door shut against the angry waves that were crashing onto the deck. When the door was finally sealed they tightened the dogs, exhausted. "Get someone to clean this up." Mitch pointed at the water that had come pouring in as he barked his orders to the boson. "Who did we lose?" Johnny knew there was no way anyone could survive out there in that storm.

"Lito!"

Johnny looked out the small window on the door.

"Why would he go out there in this? He was much smarter than that." Johnny hoped that the mate's conscience might kick in and he might say what he had done.

"You never know with these guys. Maybe he was trying to be the hero. Whatever the reason, the paper work now is going to be a pain in the ass. Not to mention the investigation will cost a fortune, you can kiss that Christmas bonus goodbye."

Johnny stared in disbelief. Any hope of decency had drained away. He never got used to the way the Filipino crew were treated. They were at the bottom of the barrel, hardly treated like humans at all. It killed him to watch them working like dogs to earn a bit of money to send home to their families yet earning very little respect in turn. Johnny wasn't high enough in the ranks to change anything so he just tried to be as nice to them as he could. But this was a total disregard for a lost life. There was surely a family with open mouths depending on his life to feed them. It could be certain that no insurance or compensation would be given. They would now be left to fend for themselves. It was all too dismal for Johnny to think about. The alarm sliced through his thoughts like a knife, reminding him that he would have to think about this later. He had work that needed to be done.

"I have to get to the engine room." Was all he allowed himself to say.

He continued down the stairs to the control room.

"Johnny, where have you been?" barked the chief. "Boiler #2 is down. Get over there before Mark makes a real mess of it."

"We lost Lito!" Johnny said.

He saw the chief's face drop a little. Johnny felt redeemed that not everyone above him was callous.

"That's a shame, but we can't worry about that now." Johnny knew that was all that would be said on the matter until they were up and running again.

He ran over to the boiler but was thrown off his feet by a powerful wave. He hit his head on the rail but got up, shook it off and continued on to the boiler. Mark was fumbling around with it.

Johnny bent to take over from the young fourth engineer; a drop of blood fell to the floor in front of him. He swept his hand over his forehead to find that he was bleeding. He would take care of it later. Johnny could see the problem with the boiler straight away; still it took him half an hour to fix it. Every minute that it was down meant the ship and everyone on it was vulnerable. He was relieved when he finally had it running again.

Johnny headed up to the bridge where he could safely view the full fury of the storm when he heard the sound that is dreaded by all engineers. The bang echoed through the engine room. Then all the machines began to shut down one by one. He ran back to the control room to get the assessment. The main engine was down, without it they had no control over the ship. They were at the full mercy of the storm. A storm that was very unlikely to show them any compassion. There was no time to waste. He needed to drop oil from the main storage tank. He took Mark with him not knowing how useful he would be but suspecting that any two extra hands would be better than none.

Johnny prayed that dropping the oil would stabilize the pressure so that they could start the engine again. With the engine dead they were being rolled harder then ever.

As Johnny arrived at the storage tank he realized that Mark was no longer with him. He glanced down the alley way and just barely caught a glimpse of him. He was in a corner retching out his last weeks dinner. Johnny ignored it. He couldn't worry about him now. He reached for the valve and tried to loosen it. At the same time a wave hit the ship and knocked him to his knees. He rose and tried again to loosen the valve. It was stuck. There was no way that he was going to be able to drop this oil alone. "Mark, get over here and help me. Now!"

The two of them strained and fought against the valve until finally it came loose and the oil started to go. They ran down the alleyway to the control room being tossed from wall to wall. They wouldn't know if this had worked until they reset the engine.

"OK, Chief, start her up."

The clicking sound was music to their ears as the engine started up again so did all the other machines. The chief called up to the captain on the bridge.

"We're up and running again. Get us out of here." That was all Johnny heard before he hit the ground.

He awoke later in the infirmary. The second mate, who was also the trained medical officer, was stitching up his forehead.

"Welcome back," he said " the good news is that you're going to live, the bad news is you're going to have one hell of a headache in the morning."

"How long was I out?"

"Long enough to miss the rest of the storm. It's smooth sailing from here to Antwerp."

Johnny said nothing. He went back to his cabin to lie down. He took the picture out and stared at his family back home in Inis Mór. He couldn't wait to get back home. In the morning, he would call his wife. His thoughts went back to Lito's family and the phone call that they would receive. He lay quietly for the rest of the night, finally allowing himself the chance to reflect.

Hunting Ducks
Imelda McFall, Rathlin Island

I always went with my Dad when he hunted ducks, rabbits as well. Our dog Sprocket used to love going hunting, but he's dead now. He was lovely. A great big brown dog who used to lick my face when he got excited. Dad always said he was a nuisance but I know he loved him. I used to see him rubbing Sprocket's big head and feeding him treats when he thought no-one was looking. Jenny used to get jealous when Sprocket would come to me instead of her, she's my sister; there are eight of us. There's Patrick and Michael, Claire and Danny. Then the twins Frankie and Maria, Jenny's next and I'm last. Jenny's my worst sister. It's probably because she's a girl. She always used to fight with me over Sprocket. She'd say "Jamsey, he's my dog!" and I would say "But Mum gave him to me." Most of the time Dad stopped us before we started to throw stones.

My Dad was a big man. He had curly brown hair, just like me and Danny. He wore a funny cap with patches on it and a peaky bit at the front. His brown coat always smelled like smoke from his pipe. Frankie smokes a pipe sometimes too, even though he isn't allowed. Him and Maria have blonde hair like Mum. I miss her, she went to heaven last year. She had lovely blue eyes and smelled like the yellow flowers in springtime. Some people say I have her eyes but I don't think so. Patrick has her eyes. Michael and he always get to go hunting on their own. They've left home now, got married. Patrick has a baby, Michael doesn't yet, but Aunty Claire, that's my Dad's sister, says he's working on it.

My sister Claire followed Dad hunting one day. He was really cross, said she spoiled the ducks, whatever that means. He was really red and shouted "Women aren't supposed to go creeping after hunters, little girls especially. They shouldn't even be going to school. You could have got yourself killed".

I think Dad must have punished her; he was cross for two days and Claire stayed out of his way. He sometimes punished me too, but only when I was bad. Frankie was bad a lot; he ran away after his fourteenth birthday, that's almost two months ago now. I don't know where he is. Maria and Jenny miss him, they keep crying for him when Dad's not around. I went looking for him for a whole week. I thought he might be down at our hidey-hole, Danny told me I was wasting my time. I kept looking but I couldn't find him anywhere. Maybe he's with Mum and Sprocket, I hope not, I miss him too.

Last time I went hunting with Dad and Danny I asked him if I could have a go with the gun. He said no. I was cross with him and kept kicking the stones along the path. Danny was laughing at me and I tried to punch him but I couldn't get close enough, his arms are too long. We walked all the way round to the far side of the big lough. Right round to the place where the rabbits have their burrows in the hill, near where Sprocket is buried. It was his favourite place. We lay down on the grass for a long time. Then the ducks appeared. I stuck my fingers in my ears. The gun is really loud and always makes me jump. After Danny killed one duck and Dad killed three and shot at some crows, he got me to run over to the other side of the low wall and pick up the ducks. That's the first time I got to do that. I could only find two of them, Dad found another one and Danny carried the gun. While Dad and Danny were looking for the last duck I was sitting in the grass examining one of the ducks' heads. It had lovely shiny feathers and its eye was still open. I didn't like the way it was staring at me, so I put it down. Another one was still warm and all wet on one side. I tried to dry it with my fingers and got all covered in its blood. I threw the duck away and ran down to wash my hands in the lough, near the long reeds, I don't like to have blood on my hands it makes me feel sick. Dad came over to me and told me to get out of the water.

"Why should you get wet feet when you can wash your hands at home."

He said that three ducks would be enough to make for a good dinner on Sunday with Auntie Claire and Uncle James, and that the buzzards could have the other one. He said he would get Maria to show me how to pluck and clean a mallard in the morning.

We started to walk back along the high ridge towards the top of our land. From there you can see right down the valley as far as the town. Dad sometimes went down into town to the pub. I'm not allowed in there. I always thought the river that runs down the hill, through the town and out into the Irish Sea looked like some kind of strange, twisty, silver ribbon from a dream or a fairytale. I was just thinking about this when Dad stopped, turned round and asked me how tall I thought I was. I was confused and asked him why. He just said he wanted to know. Then, after a while he said that if I was taller than the shotgun I could have a go. I said I thought I was and he told me to turn round. I stood up tall, on my tiptoes. I was shaking a little because there was a cool breeze and the sun was in my eyes. He measured the gun against me, I could feel the cold steel on my back. I hoped really hard that I was taller. He said "This gun was your grandfather's, you know."

"I know, Frankie told me," I said. Slowly he took the gun away from my back and started to walk on without saying anything. Danny gave me a cuff in the ear and whispered, "What'd you say that for?" I rubbed the side of my head and shrugged at him.

"I was only sayin' is all."

I didn't know what I'd done wrong. I wanted to ask Dad if I was taller than the gun but I didn't want to make him angry.

We walked along and down the slope to where the grey stone is on the hill, and stopped for a while. We always stop at the grey stone at this time of year. September's got the best sunsets, especially the last week. Dad was looking away off into the distance as if he was listening to a secret message being whispered on the wind, that only he could hear. I listened too but all I could hear was my Dad's wheezy chest breathing in and out. It seemed to get louder every time. As I sat on the cold surface of the grey stone and looked at the ground I felt really disappointed. I kicked the stone with my heels and picked at the hole in knee of my corduroys. I was cross. I thought I mustn't have been big enough yet, just like I wasn't big enough for a new bike, even though the old one's brakes were all squeaky and the front wheel was wonky where Uncle James ran over it with the tractor. It wasn't fair. I was never big enough to do anything. All of a sudden, Dad tapped me on the shoulder. I looked up at him. He was muttering something under his breath, next thing I knew he gave me the gun. I couldn't believe it. So I was big enough after all!

The gun was really heavy, Dad had to help me hold it up. Danny was laughing at me again. Dad told him to be quiet. He said it wasn't my fault I was too small and skinny for my age. Danny huffed after that and said he was going home. Dad said if he was going to be like that he could take the ducks on home too. He grabbed them and stomped off down the hill. I felt really special being allowed to touch my Daddy's gun. He said I was going to be the best hunter in all of Ireland. As I held the gun in my arms it felt big and strong, just like my Dad. Just like I was going to be. Dad helped me find the trigger and on the count of three I shut my eyes and, bang!!! I nearly fell over, the handle of the gun stuck into my shoulder and made me suck in my breath hard. It was really quite scary, but I didn't care. I had shot my Dad's gun for the first time. Dad helped me stand up straight and I could smell the gun smoke.

"Did I hit anything?" I whispered to him.

He said I should go over to the fence and find out. I ran as fast as the wind. Faster even. I nearly fell over on the stones near the fence. I started hoaking around in the grass; it was long and full of stingy thistles I didn't notice them at the time I was too busy looking for my kill. I scrabbled around on my hands and knees and a nettle stung my face. I couldn't find anything. I was starting to get angry. I could feel tears in my eyes. But I couldn't cry, not today. I wanted to give up but I knew Dad was sitting on the stone watching me. He shouted

"Go to your left".

I wiped the stingy bit of my face, got up and started to walk up along the fence. I could hear Dad laughing loudly. He started to cough then shouted "Your other left, boy."

I walked a little down along the wire and at the big post near the stile I found a great big rabbit. I was so excited. I picked it up with both hands, it was really heavy and felt cold. Not like the ducks. They are always warm when you lift them. I thought it was amazing how Dad knew exactly where it was and I hadn't even seen a rabbit at all. I ran back over to him, trying to be careful not to trip over the rabbit with my feet.

"Look what I did Dad, look what I shot!"

My Dad was so proud of me. He had a dock leaf in his hand and while I rubbed my stung face, he showed me how to carry the rabbit properly, upside-down, with its head bob, bob, bobbing along the ground. We headed for home.

After a while, when my arms were sore, he picked me up and put me on his shoulders. As we walked he said that I was growing up fast and that soon I would be a man. He said Patrick and Michael had their own families now, the girls would soon be married when they left school, Danny was leaving to go to sea and Frankie was a dead loss. He said that after Jenny left I would be on my own. He told me that it would be my job to look after the farm. He said that I would be the man of the house. I couldn't believe it!

It was getting late when we got back as far as the lane. Above the house I could see the moon, it was very small and new and there was only one star in the sky. I made a wish just like Mum taught me to when I saw the first stars at night. I wished that Frankie would come home. Dad was always so tired after working in the fields all by himself. I always made the same wish, but it never came true. I even told the tooth fairy to keep her money and bring back Frankie, but I got a penny anyhow. I was tired and hungry when we finally reached the house but I didn't let on. I knew that that night I was going to be allowed to stay up late, like a man.

Patrick, Mary and little Johnny came to visit, they said that Johnny was going to have a little brother or sister, Maria got all excited and started to jump around, Claire sent her to the scullery to make tea for everyone. Even me! Then Michael and Biddy popped in to say hello on their way home from the town. Our little kitchen was all crowded again. Just like Christmas when Mum was alive. We sang a few songs and Dad told the old stories we all loved. He talked about the summer that the old cow fell through the roof of the barn, and made Mum laugh so hard she spilled the milk and had to start all over again. And about the day that I was born when Jenny ran away because she wanted a new sister not a new brother. We all played 'finish the yarn' and Michael told jokes.

Before long it was time for them to leave. Patrick had to put Johnny to bed and Michael had to go to the cattle fair first thing in the morning. Maria and Danny went to bed to finish their homework. That left me and Dad sitting up by the fire along with Claire. She was darning socks and humming the song Mum used to sing. I was rubbing my shoulder where the gun hit me, it was sore. Dad was looking at me sidelong, he puffed at his pipe and poked the peats on the fire. Then he said he thought Claire should wash up the cups and think about going to bed. She got up and went away into the scullery, she seemed a little sad. I think she might have been thinking about Mum, or Frankie.

"Shoulder sore, son?" he asked. "It'll be nicely bruised in the morning, but worth it, 'eh?"

I looked up into my Dad's old face and smiled.

"When I grow up I want to be just like you." I said.

"Ach no son, you'll be better than me...just you wait and see."

I climbed up on his knee and snuggled into his tobacco-y jumper. I put my finger through one of the holes in it and twisted it around and around. I listened to the familiar sound of Dad's chest. Squeak in...wheeze out. Squeak in...wheeze out. Any time now he would cough again I thought, and he did. I wriggled on his knee to get more comfortable and started to think about Mum.

I must have fallen asleep, because the next thing I remember was waking up in my bed. It was early morning, and I could hear the wind blowing hard against the side of the house. I lay there listening to it and I realised that I could hear muffled voices downstairs. I got up and looked out of the dusty window. Down below in the garden I saw Auntie Claire's car and one that looked the same as the doctor's. Uncle James' tractor was there too and the priest's big Ford was splashing up the lane. I could hear baby Johnny crying. I looked over at Danny's bed but he was already up. I pulled on my trousers and jumper and went downstairs.

There were loads of people in the low room. Claire met me on the bottom step and as she pushed me into the kitchen, I heard Michael say that Frankie was on his way.

"Frankie's coming home?" I shouted excitedly and tried to push past her to get to Michael. But she wouldn't let me.

"Listen to me Jamesy." she said. "I have some news." Her voice was all shaky.

"But Frankie..." I started.

All of a sudden I had a bad feeling. I started to back away from her. She followed me and caught both my arms. She came down onto her knees and told me my Daddy had died. She told me that he had died because of his bad chest. I didn't believe her. I didn't want to. But Danny was there too and he was crying.

I ran out of the back door and into the yard. It was cold outside and I started to shiver straight away. I sat down in the middle of the yard in the mud and started to cry. Next thing I knew Frankie picked me up.

"Come on," he said "Don't cry. Sprocket will look after him. Dad's left you his gun."

He carried me back across the yard towards the house. I looked out over his shoulder at the byre door. It was open. Inside I could see my rabbit and the three ducks swinging in the wind.

Bean an Oileáin
Máirin Bean Mhic Ruadhrí, Oileán Thoraigh

A' mbíonn uaigneas ort, a bhean údaí,
Istigh ar an oileán
Nó a' mbraitheann tú uait an
Screachán,
Cúil Aodha is an Sullán
Nó an féidir liom tú a mhealladh
Ón áit san i bhfad i gcéin
Chun filleadh ar do dhúchas
Is teacht thar n-ais anseo chugainn féin

Tá blianta fada caite
Is iomaí oíche 's lá a bhí ann
Ó d'fhágas – sa mo bhaile ansúd
I measc na gcrann
Bíonn uaigneas orm cinnte
Is raghainn thar n-ais arís le fonn
Ach ní thréigfhinn anois an t-oileán seo
Dá bhfaighinn Éire's bhfuil ann.

Ó is cuimhneach liom an t-am fadó
Is mé ag rith thart cosnochta
Ag súgradh fríd na páirceanna
Nó ag fanacht ar an bpost
Le 'greenbacks' a fháil ó Mheiriceá
Nó 'parcels' téagar groí
Bheinn im 'Supermodel' ar feadh
Seachtaine
A' 'paradáil' sna gúnaí.

Och, faraor, tá an t-am sin caite
Imithe uainn go deo
Tá an comhluadar grámhar scaipthe
Ní fheicim iad níos mó
Na comharsana deasa, groíúla, geanúla
'Na measc bhí spórt is greann
Is tá mise anois i dTír na nÓg!
Oileán draíochta seo na mbeann

Oileán álainn, Oileán Thoraigh
Atá fairsing, fáilteach fial
Is nach aoibhinn duit, a chara
Más ann atá do thriall
Ní bheidh tú ag iarraidh filleadh as
Déan dearmad ar gach pian
Bí cinnte go gcaithfir seachtain ann
Nó cosúil liomsa, tríocha bliain!

The Mind of a Child
Karen Mould, Sherkin Island

Eoin looks out the window
Dreaming of whales and boats
He wants to drive a tractor
And keep pigs and goats

Questions and answers are his food
Because dreams and thoughts are all he knows
Realism and practice are things
He'll have to learn as he grows

A small world for a large mind
Not liking people in a crowd
That bubble's close to burst
He'll do his mother proud

Today he wants to play with me
Tomorrow play alone
Playschool the day after

Saturday, he'll watch TV at home

My Adoptive Life on Bere Island
Ellen Mullins, Bere Island

Many years ago I immigrated to England from East Cork, looking for work, never thinking in my wildest dreams that Bere Island would be calling me. If only I knew!!!!!.

I met my late husband Emmet who was originally from Bere Island while he was working in the coalmines and it was love at first sight. We married and came to Bere Island for a little honeymoon or so we thought. Circumstances beyond our control did not allow us to return to England to start our married life together. Living on Bere Isand full time was a complete shock to our systems.

We lived with Emmet's mother, who was very good to me, in a little farmhouse where we raised our four daughters and one son. We had no electricity for the first few years and had no running water or a toilet for many years. This was the way of life and everybody was in the same boat.

When I came to live here, there were a few small shops where you could get the bare necessities. There were only small boats in operation back then and I would go to the mainland to the little town to do a big shop which would tide us over for the next month till we went again. We had a donkey who would then oblige me by bringing home the day's purchases.

I helped my husband farm the land with the help of a horse and donkey, it was a lot of blood, sweat and tears and I loved and enjoyed every moment of it. My mother-in-law looked after the children for us as she was house bound and they gave her great comfort and company.

There was plenty of work for us throughout all the seasons of the year. In the spring we did the planting of potatoes and vegetables, in the summer and autumn we did the harvesting and in the winter months all the animals were put in the sheds, called cow houses, and hand fed hay and meal. Almost everybody on the island brought the milk to the creamery over the road from the month of May till October. At that time of the year we were up at around 7am to milk the cows and on a Sunday it was even earlier, around 5am, so we could attend mass. It was the tradition of the time that you always attended mass.

There were no such things as milking machines back then, so it all had to be done by hand. The milk cans were brought by horse drawn cart to the creamery by either the neighbours or ourselves.

Sometimes my husband used to go escalloping with other islanders. It was almost impossible to resist as we were surrounded by water and there was a great supply available.

Those who lived nearby were very good to us and we to them. If ever there was a time of need everybody would rally round and offer assistance.

My husband joined an Irish Lights boat called the "Ierne" for a short while which serviced the lighthouses around the coast. It was a very hard life due to weather conditions.

Money was scarce in those days and it was unheard of for mothers to work outside the home. Enough money was not to be made on the land so Emmet returned to England, when the children were young, to make ends meet. I had to farm the land with the help of the older children and if anything extra had to be done, I only had to ask the neighbours and they never hesitated to assist me. With Emmet away it was not easy for me and my family and I hated it when he had to return back to England after his holidays home.

Having 'the stations' in the houses was a ritual and every household took their turn. The local priest visited the home and offered mass and confessions and all the neighbours came. After mass the priest would have breakfast with the man of the house and the women of the house would see that everyone was happy and taken care of. Stations were held in the spring and the autumn and it was tradition that you went to your neighbour's house when it was their turn. Every four or five years the cycle began all over again. It is a tradition that is now dying out in this area.

Long ago there was no such thing as sliced pan, it was all home baking fresh from the bastabile, free range eggs, home made butter, fish, fresh vegetables and potatoes and fresh milk straight from the source. And are we not all the healthier for it now? We were self sufficient and proud of it.

Houses were painted on the inside when necessary and the outside was white washed. We didn't use wallpaper in those days and we certainly did not have many colour choices. We did not fuss over colours, we were just happy to make do with what we had.

Electricity arrived on Bere Island in 1957 and this began a new way of life for all. It was the gateway to a new world: ferry trips began to run more regularly, children were able to attend secondary school off the island, houses began to spring up and B&Bs and hostels were built to accommodate tourists. Running water gave us the luxury of having a toilet. We thought all our Christmases had come at once!

When all these changes began, we had to become accustomed to the new way of life. On some occasions we were able to cope better with the old then the new way. However, plugging in a kettle on a cold winters morning was a luxury as it was quick and convenient and this became the way forward.

I have heard it said that island people are a dying race – that's food for thought. I have seen lots of changes in my lifetime. My children are now all grown and some have families of their own off the island. My son now farms the land I once farmed and is living nearby with his wife and two sons.

Farming is much easier now, with all the new machinery and although there is a lot more paper work involved, or computer work, whichever takes your fancy.

I now have eight grandchildren and I have recently obtained the grand old title of great grandma of which I am extremely proud.

My two grandsons who live nearby visit me ever day and they bring joy and fun to my life. They keep me young at heart. I hope that their stories to their grandchildren will one day be as interesting as mine and yet so different!!!

Solitude
Kay Mullins, Bere Island

I am so lucky to be living in a beautiful place, Bere island just off the Beara Peninsula in Bantry Bay. My working life is governed by the moon, which controls the ebb and flow of the tides. I pick periwinkles.

I must be one of the few people not taking a handbag to work, instead I carry a white plastic bucket and net bag. I wear oilskins and rubber gloves. The periwinkles are at their best at the new moon and the full moon. I am a free spirit. I never have to clock in or clock out.

Some mornings I get up at six o'clock if the strands are early. Needless to say my breakfast is eaten in a mad rush. As the saying goes *"time and tide waits for no man"* and nowadays *"for no woman"*. I am all excited wondering what each day has to offer. It is never boring.

A rainbow is decorating the mountains across the way with its magical colours. The swans moving with grace arrive as if to say "good morning." Seagulls hover, breaking the silence, looking for fish and watching the boats pass by. They speak a language of their own.

Rocks jut out here and there and waves crash in against them. I taste the salt on my lips and smell the sea air all around me. I am safe in its scent. The wind blows in my face and my eyes water. Eye washes are free, and as a bonus my cobwebs take flight as well.

I lift the weeds to find the periwinkles. Then the tide rolls in and I imagine someone is calling it back out. It carries away gravel and sand and makes a new design with its every move.

Sometimes in a rock pool a small fish flutters frantically, splashing water about. How dare I invade its space. The crab hides discreetly until I feel its claws. I laugh as I watch him rush away on his side.

The tide turns bringing in a piece of driftwood and some debris. Broken shells battered in a storm, could tell their own story and sometimes make their way to someone's mantelpiece to enhance the beauty and wonder of another world. I'm lost in thought. I pick till the tide follows me in.

Before I realise it, my bucket is full of periwinkles and my net bag is filling up. It never seems to matter how many I have gathered, it's the experience that's the most important.

My day is coming to an end on the strand, I am contented. Whether I'm coming home with an overflowing bag of periwinkles or only a quarter full, I have been in heaven, solitude at its best.

I have been on my hands and knees for sometimes three to four hours. Someone once asked me " *are you not lonely?*" I was amazed. Even though I am all on my own I am never lonely. I am close to nature and at total peace.

People pay a fortune for medication to relieve stress related illnesses. What a shame, but it is never too late to discover the beauty that surrounds us. Natural medicine is outside everyone's door, all around the coast of Ireland and its healing properties are absolutely free.

Our Very Own Theatre Group!
Carol Murphy, Bere Island

I lie awake on the morning of St. Patrick's Day with the light stealing in through a gap in the curtains. I am filled with a warm feeling of anticipation as the Bere Island Troupe is about to perform their second Synge play, "The Tinker's Wedding" in the old army building on the island known as the Camp Church. My mind begins to wander and I wonder how did I come to be part of a Theatre Troupe on Bere Island?

When I settled on Bere Island some fifteen years ago, one of the things I missed most about Dublin was the theatre. I loved the cinema also, but there was some small compensation with films on TV, rented videos and the occasional visit to the cinema in Cork.

Ten years later there was a celebration to mark the 200th anniversary of the French Armada landing in Bantry Bay to assist the Irish rebellion under the leadership of Wolfe Tone. During the celebrations, one of the events was the production of a play about Wolf Tone's last night in prison following his arrest by the British. It was performed by a professional theatre group from Dublin in the Drill Hall in an old army building on Bere Island. It was an excellent performance and I was enthralled. Here was live theatre being performed on Bere Island! I couldn't believe it and was mesmerised for weeks afterwards.

During the celebrations to mark the opening of the Martello Tower on Bere Island I got that feeling again. A mock battle between O'Sullivan Bere and Lord Carew was staged in the open beside the Tower, almost Shakespearean in its authenticity! Several adults and many children dressed up in battle dress together with homemade swords and shields. They spoke a few words and then all hell broke loose as the battle began – I couldn't believe it – here it was again – live theatre on Bere Island!

A couple of years ago, the Bere Island Project co-ordinator arranged for Agnes Walsh, an artistic director from Newfoundland, to pay a visit to Bere Island with a view to recording the oral history of the Island. The posters read "Turning Ordinary Lives Into Theatre" – I was immediately hooked by the word "Theatre" and attended all the sessions. A year later, Pauline sourced funding for Agnes to return to Bere Island as part of the Ireland/Newfoundland partnership with the specific aim of setting up a Theatre Group. So there it was, if I couldn't go to the theatre, I could be instrumental in forming a theatre group on the Island. Following Agnes' arrival, not only did we form the "Bere Island Theatre Troupe", but we staged Synge's one-act play "In the Shadow of the Glen" after only two and a half weeks of preparation! Virtually the whole Island turned out for our first performance and it was a resounding success. We all got such a buzz out of it we were on a high for weeks afterwards. Nearly every household was very generous in giving us an amazing assortment of props and costumes.

Travelling to Newfoundland, we visited Agnes and her Tramore Theatre Troupe who are based on the Cape Shore, a rural area of Newfoundland which has remarkable similarities to Ireland and in particular, Bere Island. We performed "The Tinker's Wedding" for the people of the area and spent some time forging the links between our two communities with an emphasis on the oral history of our respective communities.

Since then our small theatre group has performed many plays to "full houses" on the island with audiences also from the mainland. We love every minute of it and look forward to whatever lies ahead of us. I know in my heart and soul that whatever it is will be exhilarating and most of all – fun!

Island Life – My Story
Margaret Murphy, Bere Island

I come from Castletownbere originally and moved onto Bere Island in 1960 for my first teaching job. I had gone to Coláiste Ide in Dingle and onto teacher training in Dublin. I was 20 when I moved onto Bere and later that year I met Finbar my husband, an islander. I fell in love with him and the island and have never looked back.

I was young and full of ambition. We married in 1962. Our first child was born in 1963 and I continued to have 6 more children, one of whom died of rheumatoid arthritis aged 3 and 1/2, a condition quite treatable nowadays.

I continued working throughout motherhood. Being a working mother was unheard of in those days but it did not bother me what people thought. I had developed a thick skin when I was young as I was brought up by a single mother, which was also unheard of. My father was a British Army man from Scotland. I do not remember him. He left my mother with 3 small children when I was about 5 years old. My mother worked her fingers to the bone as a housekeeper and cleaner and this is probably where I learned my independence. She died aged 56 of cancer and no doubt a lot of her illness was due to the stress of her hard life.

It wasn't at all easy being a working mother back then, but my neighbour would come every day and look after the children while I was at school. The school I taught in was in Lawrence Cove. After a few years I was made Principal. There were about 35 pupils then. My husband used to drive me the 5 miles east to work and back until I learned to drive, which was not very common then. I got my own car, a bubble car made for 2, but that could squeeze in 3. We took up residence in the presbytery for a year while a new school, St. Michaels, was built. This is where I remained until I retired in 1996 after being diagnosed with Multiple Sclerosis. We had between 30 and 35 children most of the years at this school. I am great friends with the Principal who took over when I retired. She travels in from Castletownbere everyday and I suppose I never realised how lucky I was to only travel over the road to work. Travelling to and from the island has become much better over the years as now you can take cars over and back. I have been in a wheelchair for the past 5 years and luckily can travel in and out in a car. I don't know how I would have managed years ago in the old punts. Life would have been very difficult.

Bringing up children years ago was a different kettle of fish. They have so much nowadays but I don't know if they are happier. When I think back how things were, lunch was a cut of 'one way' and a mug of milk, now it's something from the supermarket and a fizzy drink. We used to send the children out to play and you wouldn't see or hear them till you called them for their dinner. They used to play black den, red rover, hopscotch and they all had a skipping rope. Now you are not normal unless you have Playstation and most games are played indoors.

Farming is something else that's changed enormously in the past 60 years. There was no mower on the island until Jackie Sullivan was the first to get a mowing machine. He went around to all the farmers to cut their meadows. People used to toss the hay by hand and then make cocks of hay. These were stored in sheds. It was tough work at the time when you think back, but we just got on with it. All the family would be out saving the hay and "many hands makes light work" as the saying goes.

I used to love baking when I was able. I especially loved making sweet cakes. Creaming margarine and sugar together was lovely and the base for most things. Of course most eggs nowadays are from the supermarket. I used to have my own hens and had lovely free-range eggs. They provided plenty for our family. At first I kept a cock but they are very cross and noisy, so we just kept the hens. I also kept guinea fowl and they were great pets. I named one of them Rover and he was as good a company as a dog. Eventually a fox got him. I don't think there are many foxes left on the island, which is actually quite sad because they are a beautiful animal. Farmers killed them all. Another animal that seems to be gone is the rabbit. The disease myxomatosis came here in the 80's and over time pretty much wiped out all the rabbits, but it seems that they are making a comeback now.

I am an avid birdwatcher and nothing pleases me more than to see a flock of birds. I used to feed them everyday on my bird table. I would call them and they would come to the call. It was mostly chaffinches, which I love, but also bullfinches, robins and sparrows. I think birds are the most beautiful creatures of all. To wake in the morning and hear them singing is heart warming. I don't think people pay enough attention to the birds or to the nature around them. Even nowadays you don't see half as many butterflies as you used to see 15 or 20 years ago. So already our way of life has had that much impact. We have so much nowadays, and no doubt life is easier but are people really happier? People now are cash rich and life poor, but long ago it was completely the opposite. I think the latter is better.

Innocent Death

Margaret Murphy, Bere Island

So tell me what war is
Why should we repeatedly take
Lives of the innocent people
Surely it's their leader we hate?

Many places are governed
Under no control of their own
They have no vote, no democracy
When their countries fight they're alone

Refugees with no home or food
Left to die with no grave
Innocence in the name of death
Justice spelt with letters of the slave

Maybe practice is the way forward
Yet, can't it be resolved over a table
Rather than in some bloody battle
Please don't tell me nobody's able

The Painting Duo
Kathleen O'Halloran, Inisbofin

Over to Audrey's, I did go,
Where we would start
We did not know,
We fixed the papers
And filled the tray
And moved everything
That was in the way.

So then we were started
With paint to wall,
Praying and hoping that
None would fall.
And at last we met the door,
But ah ha, we got none on the floor.

We would stand with glass in hand
And roller dripping,
But we did not mind as long
As we were sipping,
Always red and never white
But I don't think we'd mind
On the night.

All we wanted was a job
Well done,
When having a drink it tends
To be fun,
Our time is our own so
Who cares?
Cause we both can't wait
To start upstairs.

August Boat Races, Kilronan
Nonie O'Neill, Inis Mór

Dear Triangle,
I saw you on the horizon in the morning. You reminded me of a glaziers pin. Small and sharp. Connemara was the frame. The sea, the glass. You held them together.

I forgot you till later when you and six of your relations black-swanned into Killeany pier and dozens of humans strutted and fretted and made noise in your honour.

A distraught woman brought you to my attention. She pointed down. You were lying on the cement. An unfurled wing the colour of cocoa. Five grown men knelt 'round you on hands and knees, lamenting, cursing. You, their beloved cloth triangle, could no longer hold the wind. A slash of 24 inches. Your gruff crew folded you resignedly in halves and quarters, like any proud housekeeper. They bore your heaviness aloft between them.

But, 'she' would not rest. 'Her' men must have hope. I was willing, but knew nothing about triangles.

Soon, you had flooded my entire kitchen. Like a long, muddy river, you wound through my front door, across the floor, up, over the table, knocking all my precious ornaments in your path. Finally, you gathered your wrinkled brownness through the narrows of my Singers' presser foot. The thread was red. No muddy river brown in stock. I pushed, she pulled. Singer's needle bent and crunched into your tobacco-y skin. Four lines of blood red stitching. No more gash, and you could hold the wind. For my part in your extra-ordinary recovery, I was invited into your flapping and fluttering world for 2 hours.

We left the pier, together, with your relations. All circled and wheeled and hovered like crows eyeing the same winkle. A few caws and squawks, meant to undermine. The priest pulled the trigger. All those black birds leapt and bolted out to sea. In full flight, the hush. I stood on the lumpy grey boulders at the bottom of your boats' black body. I kept looking up at you, my winged triangle. The land slipped by. I was trying to locate that lazy old red snake that slithered and wove among your brown folds. You made me feel like that Egyptian queen wrapped in her coloured carpet. You, made me feel, Triangle.

Mist

Nonie O'Neill, Inis Mór

You stand before me under the porch light
Your eyes fixed unblinking on something beyond
My shoulder in the dark.

Silver beads festoon each hair on your head.
Tiny baubles quiver, in silent want,
Most luminous, most round
Just before they fall.

The downward tug, the headlong hurtle,
To satisfy the clay, to quench the root,
To merge, to trickle, to gather speed,
To careen together on underground streams,
Through salty caverns,
To spill into the ocean.

But you are mine for this brief moment,
Between descending from a cloud and
Disappearing into a sea of others.
Now, quickly, I must marvel at your mute beauty.

Singing Gate – Kilmurvey
Nonie O'Neill, Inis Mór

Zephyr[1], my friend,
Is that you?
Was your father, Aeolias[2],
Able to keep his other five brats
Locked in the cave today?
Kicking and howling their heads off.

While, you, gentle Zephyr,
Wafted us down the green lane,
Past the calf and the primrose,
Past the pony and the pussy willows.
You wanted us to know.
You wanted to be heard.
Not like your brothers,
Whining and wailing,
Knocking and banging.
No!

You found an aluminium cattle gate,
And you played it like the pan pipes.
Low, like a tune on my B whistle.
We had to bend an ear.
But you entranced us, Zephyr, as
No human musician ever could.
We did not want to leave.

---

1 A gentle west wind
2 Father of all winds

Unfortunately,
Your father lost control of the brothers
And he let the cat out of the bag.
Which cat?
I am positively sure it was Boreas[3],
Because the next day
Knock Mordan and the Twelve Pins[4] were white
And the roads were made of glass.

But, we heard you Zephyr.
And we wait for your return.

---

3 A biting north wind
4 Mountains in Connemara

Cobwebbed
Dolly O'Reilly, Sherkin Island

That's how my heart feels –
Something in that silver network
Stops the blood flow –
Seals

An excerpt from *Island Sunday*
Dolly O'Reilly, Sherkin Island

I am sitting at the kitchen table cutting a head of cabbage for dinner. My mother is sitting opposite watching. I am forty years old and she is seventy-seven, but she is in charge of all household affairs and more active in every way than I am.

I fill a dish with water and take a bottle of vinegar from the cream-painted wooden cupboard behind me. I try to open the bottle but cannot.

"Put it in the durn of the door and squeeze,' my mother says,

I do and it opens easily. I spill some into the water.

"What's that for?"

"It's to kill the bugs in the cabbage."

"Aw, the poor creatures. I always wear my glasses and pick them out."

I roll the leaves up and chop.

"There's no need to cut it so small."

I say nothing.

"Put the green stuff at the bottom and you can have that. I find it too hard, so I'll have the white stuff."

I chop away and place the cabbage in the saucepan as instructed. I concede all points. It is her house and always will be and I am not resentful of that fact. She's not by any means a nag. Most of the time I do exactly as I want in my own space, within her space and she doesn't interfere. I am also a hard person to live with. I hardly have any patience, am barely schooled in the art of compromise and am totally spoilt from living – more or less – alone and doing as I please.

I shove the cabbage-filled pot towards her.

"You do the rest, now."

She scrapes a slab of butter off the knife into the pot and carries it to the back kitchen. The electric kettle has just boiled. I lift the lid and see white suds.

"Mother, the water is funny again. Will I boil another kettle for the cabbage?"

She hums and haws and dumps the whole lot into the pot.

"I suppose t'will hardly kill us."

Of course she is right.

We have dinner at one o clock. The cold bacon is on the table. She spills boiled potatoes into an enamel dish and spoons the cabbage onto our plates. It is delicious. I mash it up with the scalding spuds and more butter and eat two full plates.

Moving to the Island
Helen Riddle, Bere Island

One of the first things I bought when I moved to Bere Island was a pair of Wellington boots. That was a sign as to how different my life was going to be. Previously, practical footwear had never been a part of my wardrobe.

For as long as I can remember I had always harboured a dream of living on the Island. My mother was born there and since childhood my sister and I had spent every school holiday there. Moving to Bere Island was something I knew I would always do. As a child I always dreaded the holidays coming to an end and on my return to London I would start counting down the days till my next visit. At the time my goal was simple, the minute I was old enough to leave school I was packing my bags and going to live on the Island. However, the dream got put on hold due to university, travelling in the USA, and then landing my dream job working in television.

Sadly it took the sudden death of my father to make me realise that life is short and that old cliché is true, you really don't know what's round the corner. During the confusing months after my dad's death, I finally decided it was time to stop talking about it and do it. So in August 2002, I made one of the biggest decisions of my life. After ten years working with BBC News in London I handed in my notice and decided to move to Bere Island.

I had just over a month to finish up at work, sort out the logistics of the move, and then embark upon mammoth shopping trips. After all, if a shopaholic like me was to going to live on an island 90km away from a major shopping area, I needed to have everything I considered essential and, most importantly plentiful supplies of my favourite MAC lip gloss, which I'd discovered wasn't sold anywhere in Ireland.

I was faced with having to sort through my wardrobe in London and deciding which clothes and shoes would be practical for Island life, and which would have to be left behind. Well that type of prioritising just doesn't work with me, so I ended up with luggage stuffed with everything from thermals and warm fleeces to sequined sparkly handbags and cocktail dresses. I decided it was better to be prepared for all eventualities and there was always the possibility that there would be a social event on the island that might demand a sparkly handbag!

Fortunately I had somewhere to live on the island; my mother had inherited her old family home in the village, and I had been offered a job to work on a project for the Island Council. My first few weeks there were spent trying to find a home for the mountain of stuff I had brought with me and getting to grips with the new job. It also took a while to adjust to the fact that I wasn't on holiday anymore but that I was really living here.

There were days when I missed my family and friends and wondered if I had done the right thing. People had warned me that the Bere Island winters could be long and bleak. That was actually one of the reasons why I had timed my arrival for September; I thought if I could survive the winter I could take anything island life threw at me. I was kept busy with my new job, but there was a week during my first November, when it rained every day – it got dark at about 4pm and the place seemed so desolate – I seriously considered giving up and moving back to London. But for the moments like that, there were plenty that made me realise I had made the right move. Waking up on a cold frosty morning to find the field across from my house carpeted with frost, catching the ferry to the mainland the morning after a storm and watching the waves crashing alongside the boat, that was definitely a better option than travelling on the London Underground! Even walking out into my garden on a winter's night and seeing what seemed like millions of stars in the blackest of skies, something I'd never seen in the London night sky – which was always bathed in the glow of city lights.

The pace of life is definitely more relaxed here. Since moving here I've had the opportunity to do things I simply never managed to find the time for when living in a city. I've learnt to paint, play the piano and most recently, traditional Irish dancing. And for someone who's past foray into 'gardening' was buying a few bunches of flowers in Marks and Spencer every week, I'm now growing everything from roses to radishes.

I manage to visit London a couple of times a year, visits which of course include a shopping fix, although I've since discovered that I can now get MAC lip gloss in Cork City and I've even used my sparkly handbag on a few occasions! And as for those wellies, well naturally they're multi-coloured and covered in glitter.

Island Scholars on the Crests of the Waves
Kitty Sullivan Rooney, Bere Island

"Shhhh…The forecast…Listen…. Gales…What do you think?" – my father's voice wondering if it was too bad to go.

The weather forecast, that larger than life background force, determined whether or not we went across the harbour to school that day. Formative school years on Bere Island in the 1960's were like school years anywhere else in Ireland at that time, strict, predictable but secure and just a short walk from home.

At the age of 14, this safety net was abruptly torn when we had to leave the island and wrestle with that mile long stretch of water to attend secondary school on the mainland in Castletownbere every day.

Usually seven or eight *scholars*, (as we were referred to by older people), travelled in open wooden boats with an outboard engine. To reach the boat early in the morning meant a walk through the fields or a two-mile cycle up and down hills before even beginning to negotiate the unpredictable waters.

Sometimes as we skimmed over the silent calm harbour we enjoyed the sheer beauty of the landscape as the smoke rose from the various houses amongst the hills. Mornings like these seemed just perfect with the reflection of the blue mountains on the water… fragmented only by the ripples of our boat and by the thought of school!

If there were strong gale force winds we had the unexpected joy of a day off. However if it was deemed reasonably safe we often crossed, with strong winds and huge waves, flouting the danger signs. Tarpaulin was hauled over us as protection when the boat rose and fell with a thud splashing spray over the sides, soaking our shoes if we weren't quick enough to shift them!

The boys always drove the boat. It was not regarded as ladylike for girls to do so! The driver sat on the gunnell, with a carefree debonair sense of importance. Unfortunately, the boy's school opened a half an hour later than the girl's, so we were frequently late. I can still feel the butterflies in my tummy as we gingerly opened the classroom door having once again missed our English poetry lesson. The lame excuse

"The boat was late, Sister" didn't stop her from venting her anger. Children didn't dare answer back of course. Parent/teacher meetings were unheard of so problems such as these were a matter for the children to sort out as best they could.

Another area, which was regarded as problematic by the nuns, was the "undesirable" presence of French, Spanish or Portuguese fishermen in the town. Even the powers of the local Parish Priest had to be invoked to deal with this. The Canon, austere and aloof, warned us of the dangers of interacting with them in any way and stated that Convent girls were strictly forbidden to go down the pier where their boats were. As Island girls we were, of course, exempt from this and loitered on the pier waiting for our boat. We were thrilled to try out our French when they lavished attention on us.

In the insular Ireland of the 1960's these dark haired young Frenchmen with their swarthy complexions exuded an air of exoticism and danger, the rhythm of a greater sea and a wider world. They shocked and intrigued us with the magazines they gave us and, no doubt, that was their intention. No shop in Castletownbere would sell such explicit material at that time. With the aid of a French dictionary we read them with urgency and excitement and swapped them with our friends as we giggled at the back of the boat. The magazines only served to confirm what our moral superiors had implied, the need to preserve our values against the pervasive influences of those whose standards were suspect – to say the least! Such was the fun of having to go to school through the sea.

In spite of their reputation our French teacher couldn't resist the opportunity to improve her accent. An otherwise mundane school day was brightened up when a young boy from Brittany was summoned to our class. He admitted that he was a lapsed Catholic and to save his soul the Reverend Sister proceeded to teach him his prayers. I remember clearly the musical accent of that bewildered young man as he started the Hail Mary "Je vous salut Marie, plein de grace............"

Older Island people bartered for goods with these foreign seafarers when they went to town to do their shopping. After lively arguments in broken Spanish and English phrases, strong smelling cigarettes were acquired and glistening bottles of Cognac were often to be heard clanking amongst the jars of marmalade and other groceries at the bottom of the boat!

The annual regatta in the town was the most entertaining event of the year for the locals. Here again our schoolgoing experiences worked to our advantage. Whenever the engine of the boat broke down it was essential to be able to row, thereby building up our skills for the races at the regatta. Sometimes we travelled on a large barge and once when that broke down the owner was forced to drop the anchor and ride out the storm. Fortunately a passing fishing boat noticed and came to the rescue. What a thrill it was when this gorgeous curly haired local lad peered down over the side of the huge fishing boat at us. He must have felt like a brave hero as he helped pull and hoist us to the safety of the larger craft to the amusement of the crew. He certainly was *our* hero!

Of course there was the ever-present fear of drowning amongst all Islanders. One morning, as we set off for school, the sea was calm but by evening a gale had blown up and the water was white with crashing waves. We took the risk, as young people tend to do, and headed for home. The small boat crashed and bashed through the unrelenting swell of the seas. We were soaked and scared. We clung to each other in terror as we continued on this stomach-churning journey. I trembled with fear inside but when one of the girls panicked, stood up, threw off her coat and announced that she was going to swim to nearby Dinish Island, I summoned all my resources and assumed an air of calm. I grabbed both her hands and gradually persuaded her to SIT DOWN. It is amazing how in an emergency you can put aside your own fear and draw on the inner strength that you never knew you had. Fortunately it was the right thing to do but on the crest of *that* wave it was hard to tell which was the greater danger – to swim or to stay?

The Brave One
Mary Sullivan, Bere Island

How did we all fit in that wardrobe?
Our small faces white as the walls
From the fear, the anxiety, and the pain that was deep within,
Deep as us hidden within
We did not cry, we were brave,
We had to be!

The shaft of light nudging through the space where the doors connected
It threw a shadow on your withered face
That was aging as we all sat huddled
The tears cutting lines through your cheeks
I too wanted to cry,

But I was brave, I had to be!

You protected us, and kept us safe,
Assured us everything would be all right
The wardrobe held in your swallowed rage
Oh how you wanted to cry but you couldn't
You were frightened, trying to be brave

Everything quiet, so quiet,
The light fading as night falls
Hauling our faces into corners of the wood

You open the door back slowly and step
Into silence, and we follow one by one
Cygnets following their Pen

You iron our fears with the movements of your hands
With your whispers, that it is all right now
You make us tea and light the fire,
So brave, you tell us silently your strength

We sit around the flickering flames
It puts a rosy glow back in our cheeks
You look tired, we are tired,
We finish our tea and make our way to our feathered beds
You gently kiss us all goodnight

The wardrobe is now illusive
But the pain in your face lingers forever in my thoughts.

Dad

Marian Stout, Heir Island

He wasn't there. I sigh a brief statement of disappointment. I would wait for him near the window. Then I could watch the moon reflecting on the falling rain, a luminous theatre of dancing droplets. I stretch my elbows along the sill. A child once again waiting in the rain.

He never came. Sometimes I waited until it became so cold and dark, mother would force me back inside. Until the last time when I was ten and then he never came at all. Mother said it was for the best; the drink had taken his mind and had he stayed he would have taken us with him to hell.

The moon shone brighter tonight than most moons of any given night. I hear a noise from outside. A commotion, two men, sombre, darkly clad strangers enter the room. They nod in acknowledgement of me, alone in the large moonlit space. More noise, I look beyond the two large men. Auntie Agnes dressed impeccably holding on to my little cousins, Rosie and Jimmie. Other people follow unreal, ghostly, a blur in the half-light. A tall priest with a leather book folded underneath his arm walks toward me, beckoning me.

He'll be here soon. My long wait is finally over. I feel cold, suddenly free. The dark coffin is set to rest near the window. The funeral rites are read as I whisper to him beyond the moonlight, "Goodbye Dad".

Michael John's Barn
Rhoda Twombley, Inis Lyre

Michael John folded himself in half, his aching back barely allowing him the clearance he needed to pass under the barn's half-door. The upper half was closed against the wind and as he passed under he felt its wood rub against his jacket. Not an easy task for a man as tall and rheumatic as Michael John.

The old farmer stood inside the door for a few moments and gave his eyes time to adjust. The day was dark and stormy; what grey light there was snuck into the barn through gaps between the beams and corrugated roof. A narrow bit of perspex to the rear of the roof, its surface covered with cobwebs, moss and wind-blown dirt, offered little more than a dull halo of daylight. But at least it was warmer inside than out, the air thick with familiar and comforting animal smells.

His eyes lit on the pure black bull calf lying quietly in a corner on a bed of hay, legs tucked under him. He was an Aberdeen Angus and should have grown to be his owner's pride and joy. After all the nursing and handling, hand feeding and petting he was a pure dote of a beast, but only half the size he should have been. The creature lowed and dipped his head whenever he saw Michael John, nuzzling the calloused hands with a soft, warm nose. He gazed up now at the old man, his lash shadowed eyes blinking and dull in the dim light, steam rising from his nostrils as he welcomed his friend with a soft *moo*.

"Ah, Blackie, now . . . how goes it with you today my friend?" Michael John lowered himself carefully to one knee at the calf's side, fondly ruffling the fur between the bulleen's ears. Running his hand along the side of the quiet bullock, he hoped against hope that the swelling had gone down. The poor beast had been like a balloon for the past month and although the vet had inserted a valve to allow the build-up of gas to escape, Michael John despaired of Blackie's prospects.

But the old man didn't have to feel the poor animal to know he was bloated grotesquely out of proportion. Even in the pale light he could see the bulge of Blackie's side. Feeling the valve with his fingers he found that it had clogged up again. Rheumatic darts of pain shot through Michael John as he rose and walked stiffly to the upended wooden milk crate that served as a table for tools. He found the knitting needle he had left there after the last time the valve needed clearing. It had been his wife's, used in the knitting of God knows how many jumpers. Maeve wouldn't need it anymore.

The needle trembled but found its mark; trapped, foul air whooshed from the valve – the most animal of fumes. He stayed by the young bull, stroking him gently along the shoulder and flank, knowing he had eased the creature's discomfort if only for a bit. Michael John saw the warm, bovine breath as faint puffs of moist fog. Blackie's hide twitched at his touch. The old man was miles away, lost in thoughts and memories that didn't have much to do with his present companion. A sensation of warmth crept over him and, as he often did since her death, felt his wife's presence beside him, could feel the touch of her hand on his arm and, for the briefest second, a whisper of her lavender water scent. A comfort, yes – but a lonely one.

"Ah, sure, Blackie boy, what's the point? There's not much for either of us now. We're both headed for the knacker's yard one way or the other." Michael John sighed deeply. "I'm tired, Blackie. Old and crocked. An empty cottage that I can barely stand to go into ... sure, I'd be better off bunking in here with you. ..." He smiled sadly as Blackie offered a gentle, rasping lick. He absently stroked the warm head, somehow always surprised by the impossible satin softness of the furry ears. "No friends left... they've all gone...greener pastures, huh, Blackie? And no Maeve. I always thought that I'd be the first to go, Blackie," he said as he straightened up, "but sure, life don't work out like you think, does it?"

Blackie's feed nuts were stored in an old steel milk can to keep the rats from feasting on them. There was only enough left for a couple of days but Michael John shovelled a generous portion into an ancient, dented saucepan. Blackie had risen to his feet and nudged the old man again with his wet nose and broad head. The rough brushing of the curling tongue against his hand was gentle but demanding and he put the pan down for the animal.

"That's it, Blackie Boy – you eat them up. You may as well enjoy them – the vet'll be here again tomorrow to have a look. He'll take care of you. Lord knows I can't do any more." Michael John pulled down a bale of hay, yanked his well-sharpened knife from a chink in the stone wall and cut the baling strings. He loosened out handfuls of the dried, sweet-smelling grass and returned the knife to its place in the wall. A bucket of spring water had been left at the far side of the barn earlier in the day and Michael John brought that over as well, a bit sloshing out with each step.

"A drink for you, my friend. And one for me." He pulled a naggin of whisky from his back pocket and took a gulp. "Used to help, that. Doesn't make a damn bit of difference now." His hand shook a bit as he topped the bottle. Michael John slid it into his jacket pocket alongside his pipe and pouch of tobacco. Blackie slurped and gulped his way through the bucket of water. Great long strands of drool and water fell from his soft mouth.

With one swipe of his work-worn hand, Michael John cleared the top of his so-called table and sat heavily on it, nearly turning it over. He had been a powerful man before the rheumatism got a grip of him. Tall, with a broad, strong back. Even the gnarling of his hands couldn't disguise their previous strength. They were still huge; right maulers as they say, his wedding ring as snug as the day it was placed there, locked in place by his grossly swollen knuckle.

Pulling the bottle from his pocket again he managed another great swallow, wincing as it burned all the way to his gut. Michael John didn't notice his patient lowering himself back down to the floor or the winter evening light fading. This time of twilight, the end of the working day, this spell of quiet had always been his favourite time of day. He was back in the yesteryear when the barn was full of cattle and a hot dinner would be waiting for him. The deep loneliness he felt and the pain that followed his every move were not, in Michael John's mind, cause for self-pity. It was the way things were and the way things would be. He did not question the turnings his life had taken or where it was leading him. His life was what it was.

Michael John picked up a hemp rope that was lying close by. The wintry afternoon light was waning, the colours within the barn flattening to shades of grey as he worked to mend the frayed ends. The rope was sound, worked hard but treated to proper coiling over the years. Only the ends showed a touch of neglect. Sloppiness was something the meticulous old man couldn't abide. Even now, when there was no one to notice, the cottage was spotless. The habit gave him little satisfaction without his wife there to tell him to leave it alone and relax.

Rope mended, Michael John continued to fiddle with it,

practising the few old rope tricks he knew from long-ago days. Absently tying knots learned a lifetime ago as a child on the farm, not really concentrating but gently turning and twisting the line between his fingers, letting it tie the way it seemed to want to. That rope seemed to know its own mind, as if by working with it for years Michael John had taught it what he wanted it to do. After several minutes he stopped and looked down at the rope in his hands. There was a knot he had never used before, one that he would never use again. He didn't have to think about it. Michael John stood and stretched himself, then stepped to the middle of the barn, under the high rafters, taking his little table with him. One toss saw the rope over the beam and, catching the end, Michael John pulled it across to a sturdy post and tied it with two half hitches. That done, there was only one thing left to do. He went to his little bull and scratched his ears and neck, looked into the eyes that stared back at him with innocent contentment. He returned to the old milk crate, stepped up and grabbed the rope. He didn't feel the scratch of the hemp around his neck.

There was no hesitation and no doubt. No tears, no sound, bar the whistling of wind and the soft crunching of fresh hay between the little bull's teeth. It was the way things were. No note and no one there to read it. The vet would know what to do in the morning.